BECOMING ICONS OF CHRIST

T0204558

OTHER WORK BY MOTHER RAPHAELA
AVAILABLE FROM ST VLADIMIR'S SEMINARY PRESS

Living in Christ: Essays on the Christian Life by an Orthodox Nun
Growing in Christ: Shaped in his Image

Becoming Icons of Christ

Mother Raphaela (Wilkinson)

ST VLADIMIR'S SEMINARY PRESS
YONKERS, NEW YORK 10707
2011

Library of Congress Cataloging-in-Publication Data

Raphaela, Mother.
    Becoming icons of Christ / Mother Raphaela (Wilkinson).
        p.   cm.
    ISBN 978-0-88141-391-5
    1. Christian life—Orthodox Eastern authors.   I. Title.
BX382.R34 2011
248.4'819—dc23

                                                            2011044788

COPYRIGHT © 2011

ST VLADIMIR'S SEMINARY PRESS
575 Scarsdale Rd, Yonkers, NY 10707
www.svspress.com
1-800-204-2665

ISBN 978-0-88141-391-5

All Rights Reserved

PRINTED IN THE UNITED STATES OF AMERICA

CONTENTS

GOD HOLDS US

God holds us
    in His fiery hands
    forever,
burning out the evil
    like impurities from gold.
We rest there
    (not a job we do ourselves),
carried right into His Kingdom.

Why think of burning passion?

It smolders only feebly
    in the Face of Love.

Chapter One

BECOMING ICONS OF CHRIST'S PEACE

"*B*ECOMING ICONS of Christ's Peace." The phrase has a nice ring to it! Yet what does it really mean? I would like to take a closer look at these words, singly and together.

We all like icons—they are so holy, so attractive. They make our Church beautiful, taking the fleshly reality of life, even the horror of the Cross of Christ, and making it into something we can gaze upon with enjoyment. Even non-Orthodox like to use icons as decorations on their walls and are led into prayer before them.

Of course we all want to become icons! Have people see us all scrubbed up, without all the warts and sin of our real lives. Bestowing blessings by our very presence.

Now let's go on to the word "peace." Peace is so wonderful. Something we rarely know well. Perhaps for some of us, it is the reason we come to Church—to find some little oasis in the midst of our lives that are chaotic, disturbed, angry, and to have some assurance that there is a reality different from the one we live with daily both in our personal lives and as members of the human race here on this suffering, terrorized earth.

Next we go on to what modifies peace in our phrase: the peace is "Christ's."

As Christians, we know that in some way or another, we are to become "one with Christ." We are to participate in His divine nature, become God or attain *theosis*, as St. Peter and the saints of the Church put it. And further, as St. John tells us in his first letter, we are also in some way to "walk as He walked," to take not only His divine, but also His human life as a pattern for our own.

9

So I want to look at His life with you, share some of the ways I have come to see Him as I have tried to pray my way through reading the Scriptures, the writings of the saints, and travel to the Holy Land. I am also indebted to two books written by the late Bargil Pixner, a Roman Catholic monk who spent most of his life in the Holy Land: *With Jesus through Galilee* and *With Jesus in Jerusalem, His First and Last Days.*

If we know anything about the life of Jesus, we know it was not peaceful in the sense that we mostly like to think about peace. He was born into a first-century Palestine that was similar to contemporary Palestine: it too was occupied by armed troops, and defended by fanatics who would go to any extreme of murder and rebellion to attempt to gain independence.

Nazareth, where he grew up, is thought by many scholars today to have received its name from the Hebrew *Netzer*, meaning root as in the Root of Jesse. It was settled by exiles returning from the Babylonian captivity who knew their royal genealogy and used that same word *Netzer* as sort of a nickname for themselves. They could not afford to live lives that would attract attention. Unlike neighboring Cana, where houses were built above ground, the people of first-century Nazareth lived in caves carved into the rock—a bit like Hobbits. They were poor, they labored, they prayed and they hoped. They did this so deliberately that those outside truly could not see their lineage: "Can anything good come out of Nazareth?"

Very recently, excavations have also revealed extensive Roman Baths there from this same period. While the full implications of this discovery are not yet understood, there seems to be little question that as poor as the villagers were, they were also host to a large Roman garrison. This emphasizes Matthew's statement: "But when he [Joseph] heard that Archelaus reigned over Judea in place of his father Herod, he was afraid to go there, and being warned in a dream he withdrew to the district of Galilee. And he went and dwelt in a city called Nazareth . . ." (2.21–22). Here we may see a positive side to Roman occupation: the family of Jesus would not be bothered by petty tyrants living in Jerusalem.

Nazareth bought them a kind of peace, space to live in and to grow. When events brought them to Bethlehem, they sought out the same sort of dwellings: caves in the ground.

We must understand the intensity of this life lived in an oasis of peace. Jesus was formed by it. He was disciplined by the training and work of a craftsman (a better translation than "carpenter," as it seems that He and His earthly father worked in stone as much as in wood). He was disciplined by being one of the poor — while knowing that his heritage was the royal heritage of both the Son of Man and the Son of God. He was disciplined by prayer and the repetition of the Law, the Psalms and the Prophets. He was disciplined by the silence and the rugged beauty of the Holy Land, where travel by foot or even by donkey was arduous, where green pastures and still waters gave way seasonally to the barren and often hostile desert wilderness, where the sea that gave food could just as easily and quite suddenly, without warning, kill. He may have learned from His parents of their escape from the deadly attempt on His life in Bethlehem that led to the slaughter of other innocent children (Mt 2.16–18). He was aware that He had spent some of his early years a fugitive in Egypt.

In the fullness of time, He walked out of the oasis of Nazareth, already familiar with the long journey to Jerusalem, knowing the pull of His Father's House, having mingled with the crowds enough to know the corruption and hypocrisy of the religious leaders who claimed to know the way of righteousness.

That was the end of the most peaceful period of His life. He walked out of Nazareth to be baptized by John and be tempted by Satan in the wilderness. He walked out to challenge directly the evil one and all of his demonic forces—and to force men to choose between His Kingdom, the Kingdom of His Father, and the kingdom of the devil.

There are some peaceful scenes in the Gospels from the brief period of His years of ministry, but as we read them through, we are constantly aware of the backdrop of challenge and warfare. In St. Luke's Gospel, the Beatitudes are followed by the long list of "Woe to you" warnings to the "scribes, Pharisees and hypocrites." In St. John's Gospel, the wonderful feeding of the crowds in the wilderness is followed by immediate disillusionment on the part of many of his followers and then at once the statement: "After this Jesus went about in Galilee; He would not go about in Judea, because the Jews sought to kill Him."

Nor does He challenge men and demons passively. We sense His incredible energy as He chooses to heal on the Sabbath and, further, in spite of the direct Sabbath prohibition, make clay out of spittle to do so; He makes a whip out of cords and drives the money changers from the Temple. After moving from His childhood home and making Capernaum something of a home base, He returns to Nazareth only to goad His own people until they rise in a murderous mob to try to push Him off a cliff. He is directly responsible for the death of an entire herd of pigs; He blasts a fig tree; He deliberately humiliates a woman who comes asking for her daughter's healing before He gives in to her request. The list goes on and on. This is not peace or pacifism as we usually think of it.

In fact, Jesus is quoted as saying: "I did not come to bring peace, but a sword." Yet what is this sword? We know from the writer of the Epistle to the Hebrews that the early Church believed the Word of God was like a "two-edged sword." Jesus Himself is that sword; that "weapon of peace." As violent as His words and actions could be, they brought healing and freedom. He is like the surgeon who knows that in some cases unless he cuts out the cancer the patient will die. And then, suddenly, everything changes. Instead of hiding in Galilee, He returns to Jerusalem. He says "My time has come," and "sets His face" to accept the consequences of His challenge to the evil one and all within his kingdom of earthly, temporal power. He tells Judas to do what he has to do "quickly."

We all know the story of His betrayal, crucifixion and death. Yet we can enter into the events of that story over a lifetime of Holy Weeks and still not reach the depths of understanding.

In the Passion of our Lord God and Savior Jesus Christ, the meaning of all that went before is revealed. The things we, together with all mankind, have thought we saw and understood, both in the writings of the Old Testament and in the life of Jesus, are finally turned right side up. Now Jesus no longer hides Himself from men. He allows Himself to be publicly judged and humiliated. He does not goad His accusers—if He speaks at all, it is to make simple statements of fact. He allows men to attack His Person—not just verbally, but physically. He places Himself in the center of that Test He tells us to pray to be spared. His human nature is pushed on every level beyond the limits He can endure. I will not rehearse the physical, emotional and psychological tortures of the Passion. Please God, every one of us has been in situations where we have been moved by the sufferings of another. It is the remembrance of such passion that allows us to be moved by the Passion of Jesus—to understand that any physical, outward suffering shows only the very thin surface of reality.

What we have to come to see, if we are to enter into the life of Christ, is the heart of that suffering. We have to come to understand the love that knows when the time has come to lay down all defenses, to be open to all the attacks of men and of demons. We have to be ready to embrace the pain of total rejection, misunderstanding, the agonizing loss of all we have worked to accomplish on this earth, for the glory of God. We have to be ready to have our faith, the very ground of our being, torn away from us, as we seem to be abandoned by all we have believed in. "My God, my God, why have You forsaken me?"

And we have to understand that this is not something we can do. We cannot begin to grasp, let alone emulate, the full extent of the Passion of the only sinless One. So often we have created our own suffering, not through righteous words and actions, but through our own stubbornness, stupidity and sin. We know how often we not only need to forgive, but to ask forgiveness. We know how damaged we are, not only by our own personal sinfulness, but by our fallen nature, so that very often we do not respond appropriately to what we experience of others and the world around us.

Yet if we are to become icons of Christ's peace, this is exactly what we are called to do. "If anyone would be my disciple, let him deny himself and take up his cross and follow me, for where I am, there also will my disciple be."

When we find ourselves in our own times of passion, or when we are faced with the passion of others, we have only one way open to us to respond appropriately, and that way is through prayer. What is impossible for man is possible for God. It is impossible for us to respond appropriately unless we ask Christ to enter our lives, to teach us to pray, and Himself to come, live and pray within us.

This way of entering into the life and Passion of Christ is the only way to His Resurrection—our own personal transfiguration by the life of God. And only as we are thus transfigured will we become icons—not icons of our own righteousness and suffering, nor of our own strength, virtue, truth and courage, but icons of the love, the power and the peace of God.

Chapter Two

OUR WARFARE

*W*E FIND OURSELVES on a highway with the rest of humanity in the midst of murky darkness compounded by human war, rumors of wars, violence and terrorism—not to mention natural disasters such as ice storms, floods, fires, tornadoes and earthquakes. A couple of generations ago it might have taken days, weeks or months for news of such disasters to reach us—unless they took place in remote areas we would never know about.

Today, however, we are bombarded constantly with documentation of horrendous situations from (to us) the most obscure corners of the globe. How can we live with this? How has the world suddenly gotten so dark?

Students of history and geology know that the earth was never a place of complete peace and rest. Yet, there are times when it seems as if some greater mass insanity takes over entire groups of people, and all the rules of civilized behavior are trampled under foot along with those who try to uphold them. "Cry 'Havoc!' and let slip the dogs of war" is Shakespeare's description of this phenomenon (from *Julius Caesar*). Deuteronomy gives us Moses quoting the Lord: "For a fire is kindled by My anger, and it burns to the depths of Sheol, devours the earth and its increase, and sets on fire the foundations of the mountains. And I will heap evils upon them; I will spend My arrows upon them; they shall be wasted with hunger, and devoured with burning heat and poisonous pestilence; and I will send the teeth of beasts against them, with venom of crawling things of the dust. In the open the sword shall bereave, and in the chambers shall be terror, destroying both young man and virgin, the sucking child with the man of gray hairs" (32.22–25).

Beginning with Jesus Christ, the Church has called this mass insanity "demonic." Those who have lived through the violent storms of nature often become aware of something that feels almost like a malevolent personality, sweeping all before it. These storms of humanity are very similar. During times of war, even those who are not directly involved in armed combat at the front will be caught up in amazing behaviors. Families and friends can be split by agonizing, heart-felt differences. Mobs can be driven in opposing directions; pacifist individuals and groups can become as violent as the military forces they demonstrate against.

These same demonic storms can overtake smaller groups even within the Church: parishes, monasteries, jurisdictions, national churches can be split into warring factions. I remember being contacted by people from both sides of a divided parish. Each would begin the conversation by talking about exactly the same things: blindness, unethical behavior, disobedience, breaches of trust and faith, etc. It might take several minutes before I could tell from the conversation which side of the split this particular person was on. Each side saw the other as being what St. Paul described in 2 Thessalonians: "Therefore God sends upon them a strong delusion, to make them believe what is false" (2.11).

In the middle of such conflicts, phrases such as "He/she is crazy!" "They have to be insane!" "How can any normal person possibly believe/do/say that!" are frequently heard. People feel driven by their honor to defend what appear to them to be life-and-death situations. And, in truth, such situations exist. It was not better when people refused to get involved and turned a blind eye to the systematic genocide of Stalin, Hitler and others, thus becoming passive accomplices in the murders of millions of people. "Am I my brother's keeper?" is a question that has been asked down through the ages.

Yet St. Paul reminds us: "we are not contending against flesh and blood, but against the principalities, against the powers, against the world rulers of this present darkness, against the spiritual hosts of wickedness in the heavenly places. Therefore take the whole armor of God, that you may be able to withstand in the evil day, and having done all, to stand. Stand therefore, having girded your loins with truth, and having put on the breastplate of righteousness" (Eph 6.14).

Many of us know that it is far easier to sit back and analyze what seems to us to be the insane or criminal behavior of others than to deal with our own personal demons. The fight is not less intense; the psychic pain can in fact be greater. Yet, unless we are willing to face and fight our own personal demons, we may well become the people the Lord speaks about in Luke's Gospel: "Or how can you say to your brother, 'Brother, let me take out the speck that is in your eye,' when you yourself do not see the log that is in your own eye? You hypocrite, first take the log out of your own eye, and then you will see clearly to take out the speck that is in your brother's eye" (6.42).

A note in the journal *In Communion* of Father Alexander Webster's book, *The Pacifist Option: The Moral Argument Against War in Eastern Orthodox Theology,* indicates that in the Church there are two accepted paths that one may take in the face of violence: One is "the path of radical pacifism, characterized by the moral virtues of non-violence, nonresistance, voluntary kenotic suffering, and universal forgiveness . . . " The other path, of defending others but never defending oneself, is described in two essays published in Paris in 1929 in *St. Sergius Leaflets.* After pointing out that a surprisingly large proportion of the saints and willing martyrs for Christ have been soldiers and military officers, it states: "The armed forces of Byzantium gave any talented and brave man the opportunity—given some luck—to make a career, but they provided something else as well: Its hardness and severe discipline were rooted in the great and deep ideals of patriotism, self-sacrifice, duty and religious feeling which, even if misguided, are still planted in the soul of man by God. . . . When defending the state, the Christian soldiers raised their threatening swords, yet these experienced fighters would not even raise their unarmed hands to defend themselves."

St. Pachomius, recognized as one of the first founders of communal monasticism in the fourth century, became a Christian while a soldier in the Roman imperial army. He went on to plant the same ideals, which produced so many military martyrs, in the hearts of his monastics. Only those willing to strive with themselves first, to subdue their own demons through prayer, fasting, obedience and the other disciplines of the ascetic life, can be true soldiers for Christ in any arena.

But can Christians today even in monasteries, let alone parishes, hope to take on such asceticism? The answer to this question could be an entire essay in its own right. Here, let us just say that the answer is yes, if we are willing to make choices—and look at the choices that we already live with, often unconsciously. We choose daily to submit to the media around us, from computers and televisions on down to Muzak and video games; we choose to say that the demands of our frenetic society are more important than our life in the Church. It is not lack of ability that keeps us from becoming saints, it is the inability to see that we have choices; that no one holds a gun to our heads to force us to sit at the computer or in front of the television for ridiculously long hours or to stay away from time with our families and children or to avoid gathering as the people of God. We need balance in our lives, so we can use our technology and enjoy our society, not be taken over by them.

May we so strive that we may be free to answer God's call to sanctity—whether it leads us through the ways of peace beginning with those who surround us, or whether it be at least during some periods of our lives, the way of public service, including "military service, the essence of which is not to kill but to offer one's life as a sacrifice for one's society, killing enemies merely out of necessity, for we are of God, and the whole world is in the power of the evil one" (1 Jn. 5.19) (quote from *St. Sergius Leaflets*, Paris, 1929).

Note: I am indebted to the website www.incommunion.org *for* The St. Sergius Leaflets *and the review of Father Webster's book posted Monday, October 18, 2004.*

Chapter Three

BOUNDARIES AND BRIDGES

Part I: Boundaries

*M*OST OF US HAVE HEARD the proverb "Good fences make good neighbors." This concern for boundaries is an ancient one, and not confined to human beings. Animals both wild and domestic set up territories for themselves with clearly defined boundaries that they may even defend to the death. The sense of "boundaries that cannot be passed" is a Biblical theme as well, where even land, sea and air are seen as separated by God with boundaries when He created the world from nothing (Gen 1; Ps 104).

Creation is an ordered affair: the entire universe has "laws" of distinction which form the basis for the whole of modern science. It is not surprising to discover that the first scientists were deeply religious people who believed in just such laws and boundaries and that some of the best contemporary scientists continue to be so as well.

Partly, perhaps, to reinforce this sense of boundaries, the Old Testament set up many rules against mingling: Plant only one crop in a field; do not weave a mixture of linen and wool; do not remove a neighbor's landmark (Lv 19.19; Deut 19.14, Hos 5.10). And indeed, the uniqueness of human beings set in their own environment, apart from other creatures, living as individuals, families, communities, ethnic groups, nations is spelled out in many ways in most of man's religions.

All of these boundaries create a livable environment for our existence. The life of a human being thrust alone without protection into the midst of a tornado, blizzard, tidal wave, earthquake or wildfire, let alone a jungle, a howling mob or the vast reaches of outer space, will be snuffed out quickly.

Perhaps greatest of all is the boundary God placed between Himself and His creation. Since the rebellion of Adam and Eve when He cast them out of the Garden of Eden, placing a cherub with a flaming sword to guard the gate, "Man cannot look upon the face of God and live" (Gen 3; Ex 33.20). The story of the Tower of Babel (Gen 11.1–9) is a tale of men taking the raw materials of creation to build a proud assault against this boundary. Today we find ourselves living once more in such a cultural building, where God Himself is challenged and questioned, along with any limits and boundaries seen to be of His placement: If a technology exists, there are those who feel they should use it, no matter what boundaries and laws of nature, ethics, love, nation, community and family may be destroyed in the process. We see terrorism, mass extinction, global warming, and nature's own forces of destruction as the first signs that this modern tower of Babel, this inability to recognize and respect the boundaries between God and fallen man, will fall as surely as have all of its predecessors.

Human history is made up largely of following the growth, development, stunting and at times brutal destruction of boundaries—boundaries that begin with the first self-awareness of an emerging nation, a new group, an infant, the realization that one is no longer simply an extension of one's parent.

On the level of churches, nations, communities, indeed any human group, adults who do not develop a healthy sense of boundaries, which includes almost all of us in this fallen world, create all of the sins catalogued in the Old and New Testaments. Those in authority may be tempted to see the people under them, even their own children, simply as extensions of themselves, who exist to serve them as their own hands and feet serve them, while often being less responsible, respectful and careful with the people than they are with their own hands and feet. Those not in authority, especially in a democracy, may have a similar temptation, seeing those elected to positions of responsibility to be likewise extensions of themselves, with the expectation that they will please them and carry out their will in every way. Given the myriad and conflicting expectations of different political parties, not to mention interest groups and individuals, God Himself would not be capable of pleasing everyone, even if He were to decide it was appropriate, which so far He has not.

Nevertheless, we do hear Christ saying that those who are in authority or "the greatest," are to be the servants of all (Mt 20.26; 23.11). I have no intention of denying this. Yet sometimes it seems as if we the people decide, therefore, that this means we can take on the role of abusive judges and masters. It is appropriate for everyone at times to follow the instructions of others, to allow him or herself to be trained, "discipled." None of us, however, master, comrade, servant or disciple, will be able to accomplish our best if we cannot as adults take responsibility for our own actions, perceptions and strengths. Wise masters gave even slaves the authority and tools to carry out work and obligations. There is a saying that peoples, communities, and groups get the leaders they deserve and vice versa. I believe there is real truth to this. Both leaders and people can enable each other in irresponsibility, corruption, and abuse; hobble each other into crippling inactivity, or, more rarely in today's culture, inspire each other to greatness.

On a more intimate level, far too many of us have experienced the phenomenon of families without proper boundaries between members. All sorts of abuse, physical, verbal, and emotional may go on when each person is seen as part of the undifferentiated family "persona." The only "boundary" that may not be broken is that which shields this familial persona from the world: In public, everyone must act as if everything is perfect. Members of such families often have an outstanding presence when they are in public, away from their families. They have a sense of needing to "keep up the image" and have the perfect family veneer that allows them to be charming, warm, compassionate, loving, and considerate to all on the outside. While it is good that they have this side, this behavior creates incredible pressure on those caught within the family: If a person tries to break out of the family secret, "blow the whistle" on what can be in some cases even brutal, criminal behavior, not only will the family retaliate, ridiculing them, accusing them of being vicious slanderers, for example, outsiders will reinforce this as well, having seen only the wonderful external persona of individual family members and "knowing" that such "nice" people couldn't possibly behave in any other way. It is a well-known phenomenon amongst "Twelve Step" groups that often the spouse and children of an addict may seem crazier in public than the addict himself. The addict is able to switch behavior on and off instantaneously, often leaving the other family members to appear to be fuming and hysterical to an outsider who walks in and very naturally comes to the conclusion that this lovely, sensitive, charming person is being "driven to drink" or some other dysfunctional behavior by his or her obviously and inexplicably angry spouse and family.

One who marries into such a family is in for a nasty shock. Until he or she is seen by the others as officially and irrevocably one of the family, the sick, abusive family behavior may never manifest itself. In literature, especially about the nineteenth century, this is a classic theme: The sheltered, sweet Victorian bride who has experienced only sweetness and light, discovering on her marriage night that she has entered a nightmare, without the ability to wake up and escape.

Communities and religious groups can fall into this same type of behavior. We reflect on the Lord's well-known accusation: "Woe to you, scribes and Pharisees, hypocrites! For you traverse sea and land to make a single proselyte, and when he becomes a proselyte, you make him twice as much a child of hell as yourselves" (Mt 23.15).

And the reverse may happen: a relatively healthy, peaceful and happy family or group may be joined by someone who perhaps even unknowingly projects their own abusive standards and behavior onto those he or she is with. We can see this in monasteries as well. Often, people who come from abusive backgrounds may not be aware that they have these "two sides," for denial may have been the only tool they had as children to survive even physically in such an environment. These people appear wonderful and charming as visitors and perhaps even for their entire period of probation. Whenever they begin to feel secure in their community position, however, things begin to change. While guests and outsiders will still see the wonderful person, the community will begin to see an irrational display of depression, anger and jealousy, normally accompanied by accusation of others, since such a person has been formed truly to be blind to him or herself. I remember being told by a wise old nun when I first entered the monastery that every time I was bothered by observing what seemed to me someone else's wrong words or behavior I was probably seeing in them what I was not willing to see in myself, to the extent that they might not even be thinking, saying or doing what I thought I felt, heard and saw: I was projecting what I would be thinking, saying and doing if I were in their position. I have learned since that this wisdom is straight from the Desert Fathers. This ability to project is even worse than the proverbial halitosis: Even your best friend won't tell you and you certainly can't see that you are doing it yourself!

Until we are able to learn proper boundaries, we build instead the walls of our own prison. When we do not love ourselves enough to accept our own healthy boundaries and limitations along with our many gifts and talents, we cannot love others properly, either. Proper boundaries allow us to see another person with true detachment—and love. Without them, we will tend to swing between two extremes: we may feel totally "at one" with others; see them simply as extensions of ourselves, when they behave as we feel they should; or when they speak or act in ways that cause us to feel threatened, we will feel totally alienated, needing to defend ourselves with ever greater physical, emotional or spiritual barriers. When others try to live with us, they soon realize that they have no clues as to what "set us off" that time. They begin to feel as if they are in a mine field, never knowing when the next step will explode yet another bomb, while we will be feeling all the while misunderstood, frightened, angry, and unable to face what we may unconsciously fear as hugely destructive forces within ourselves.

This is where blind trust and obedience can be life-saving for us. Some of us literally cannot see where we end and another person begins. May we be given the grace to pray to begin to see this blindness of ours; to begin to accept at least some of what others tell us of their own vision. We need to find at least one other person whom God has led to health and trust them as blindly as we have followed our own destructive path, even when that person's words may seem to strike at the very roots of our own sense of self and identity. Such a healing process should not last forever, but it will need to last as long as our blindness, at least in this area, exceeds that of our guide. I believe it is good to seek such a healing process, although we should use every possible means first to be sure that we are truly choosing a doctor, not a patient; a ship's captain, not just a sailor, as St. John Climacus says of finding a monastic guide in *The Ladder of Divine Ascent* (Step 4:6). While it is wonderful when we can find such a guide or mentor in our community, parish or church, we should seek out such a person wherever he or she may be found. That person need not be an authority in every area of our life—we may not need their training in theology, choir directing, bread baking or writing essays—but we do need to accept that in those areas where we are still "babes in our thinking," as St. Paul says (1 Cor 14.20), we must humbly start from the beginning.

The ability to begin thus to reach out in a healthy way, to build godly bridges that in eternity will cross over boundaries to unite people, churches, nations in the unity of the Kingdom of God will be the topic of the second part of this essay.

Chapter Four

BOUNDARIES AND BRIDGES

Part II: Bridges

*W*E, WITH THE WHOLE of creation, are fallen. Along with the writers of the Old Testament, we can take that for granted. Scandal, corruption, violence, betrayal—that whole list should not surprise us in ourselves, in others or in our surroundings. Our surprise and joy are found as we discover the Gospel faith that God meets us where we are; builds bridges over the walls of brick we have constructed around ourselves in our fallen attempts to live our own lives in spite of others (including God) and by these bridges, brings us to eternal life and salvation in the Kingdom of Heaven.

This Gospel faith—this bridge-building by God—is what we call revealed religion. One who has experienced such a revelation cannot deny it; one who has not experienced it cannot begin to comprehend it. "Flesh and blood has not revealed this to you, Peter, but my Father in heaven . . ." There is a uniqueness in revelation: a choosing and a calling. "You have not chosen me, but I have chosen you," Christ says to His followers (Jn 15.26).

If God has touched us in this way; if we have experienced something of Him through His calling of us, we will know that "our ways are not His ways" (cf. Is 55.8). The experience of the Christian saints down the ages has been that we cannot look at ourselves to experience what we are to be like, but to God in Whose image and likeness we are made.

Yet to look at God is to enter the realm of poetry. The saints who used many words to speak about Him remind us that there are no words adequate to Him: Whatever we may think or say, His reality remains far greater and beyond our grasp. When we think He fits into our intellectual constructs, we have rather produced an idol which He will delight in destroying. Many people's loss of faith is actually a step in the right direction—their god was too small and its destruction is sometimes the first step towards a relationship with the true God and Father of our Lord Jesus Christ.

One of the main reasons for the crucifixion of Jesus was that those around Him could not accept that God could or would use a man to build a bridge with His creation. God could not be walking in their midst; to claim to be God as Jesus did, was, at best, lunacy; at worst, blasphemy.

Indeed, it took Christians over 300 years to begin to come up with language to describe their experience of God's revelation in Jesus. Then as now, Christians have begun with the reality of the three different persons, with the fact that men and women have experienced Jesus, known Jesus. With the apostles, they have heard Jesus pray to His Father and speak of the Spirit as totally other than Himself: "My Father, if it be possible, let this cup pass from me; nevertheless not as I will but as You will . . ." (Mt 26.39). "But when the Counselor comes, whom I shall send to you from the Father, even the Spirit of truth, who proceeds from the Father, He will bear witness to me" (Jn 15.26).

At the same time, with Peter and with Martha of Bethany, they have come to see Him as "the Christ; the Son of God" (Mt 16.16; Jn 11.27). With the apostle Thomas they have come to an overwhelming realization that He is their Lord and their God (Jn 20.28).With the Theologian, they have heard Jesus speak to Philip and say "He who has seen me has seen my Father" (Jn 14.9). They are aware that Jesus said "I and my Father are One" (Jn 10.30).

At first, they weren't sure how to describe all this in what we today call the language of theology. There were too many paradoxes;

too many facts they could not deny yet which did not fit their view of reality. Indeed, as we continue to grow into our life in Christ, each of us goes through the same process of breakdowns in what we believe.

We do believe that God is love and that it is the nature—not just the choice—of love to pour itself out on the other. For this reason we believe God must have others as part of His very being. While some might say that Creation is the other, we believe that creation mirrors what already exists within God Himself, Trinity in Unity. This mirrors our view of human persons made in the image and likeness of God: the unity of humanity does not compromise the uniqueness and integrity of persons; true bridges do not violate boundaries.

Another image of God's revelation—His bridge-building with His creation—is found in the Biblical theme of love and marriage: In the Old Testament, *The Song of Songs* and the marriage of the prophet Hosea are examples of this allegory of the nature and love of God. St. Paul is explicit about this marital theme in the New Testament as well (for example, Eph 5.31–32). To use words of theology: In love, God begets the Son and sends forth the Spirit. Creation is seen by some as a mysterious result of the union of the Divine Son and the Spirit, just as the marriage of a man and woman normally results in the begetting of children. Nevertheless, there is a very long debate on the nature of this union that goes back at least as far as Origen and that has not yet been resolved. Some, with Origen, have taught that intercourse between Adam and Eve was only a result of the fall; that before then, the unity they had with one another in the Garden of Eden precluded sexual relations. Those who favor this approach still teach that Christians should not have sexual relations except as a matter of catering to weakness and then only to beget children.

There is another equally venerable and Orthodox reading of Scripture, however, which teaches that human intercourse was part

of God's original plan; that love indeed always pours itself out and is
by nature creative. In this view, the union of a man and woman in
marriage reflects the joining of God to His creation, i.e. the "other"
who is created and then redeemed to share in the essence of God in
theosis, without being destroyed personally. Marriage is seen as a
matter of mutual support, love and respect. If children are given in
response to such sharing it can only be a blessing. While a choice not
to bear children could be sinful depending upon the reasons, to participate in God's love and creativity can mean an infinite number of
other things as well.

When Christian marriage (and community life) shows such a
reflection of the love of the Trinity, unity is found in the harmony of
differences. Even people who are close enough to know pretty well
what the other is thinking and anticipate reactions and behavior, will
continue to be strong individuals, not pretending that boundaries
don't exist or trying to obliterate them. Such families, communities
and friendships will indeed be fruitful and rejoice as their offspring
grow up, move on, become their own persons. They expect them to
do different and perhaps even greater things than they themselves
are doing, and they understand that the main heritage they have
given them is life in the Church, the Body of Christ.

The Church as well rejoices in her offspring: new missions,
monasteries, national churches. Each of these groupings, when it is
truly animated by the Holy Spirit, reflects the uniqueness of its time
and place as well as the particular people who are called to be part of
it. When the first assembly in Jerusalem saw that the gentiles who
before were far from the Church had received the same Holy Spirit,
it recognized that this new situation called for an entirely different
framework if the Body of Christ was to flourish with these new
members. The Church, speaking through St. James of Jerusalem,
refused to place on them the full burden of the laws and traditions

of Judaism (Acts 10–11). Thus was laid the groundwork for the unique, autonomous national churches, which have ever since characterized the Orthodox Church, with a worldwide apostolic hierarchy descended from that assembly in Jerusalem balancing the local authority within the boundaries of each group.

For us fallen people, however, ignoring and violating boundaries comes naturally; building bridges does not. While as St. Paul tells us, God has been revealing Himself through His creation from the beginning of time (Rom 1), our natural fallen response is not to use creation as such a bridge to God, but rather to idolize it; to turn it into an end in itself. This is one of the chief reasons Jews and Christians have needed to place appropriate boundaries between themselves and others, so as not to lose their identity as God's "Chosen People"; not to bow down in worship to the surrounding society or its false gods.

Yet how do we reach out to others without losing what we have to share with them? How can we make sure we are not used by those things which are meant to be used by us?

Forgiveness seems to me to be the key. Without a truly robust understanding and practice of forgiveness, Christian life is a sham, whether in marriage or community. Forgiveness cannot be something tacked on after all else fails; it is the way Christians approach life, for it is the way our God approaches us. Forgiveness means being able to look clearly at the world and those around us in true detachment, seeing that all is not well (even within ourselves), and loving in spite of that. It does not mean going through life in denial that anything is ever wrong, nor in being scandalized when it becomes obvious that evil has been perpetrated by known individuals.

Such a life of forgiveness demands letting go of control—or the illusion of control—that revenge and constant defensiveness bring.

It is the way to be sure that we build bridges rather than fortifications and not violate or ignore boundaries.

Forgiveness is truly life-giving. Only one who has been truly seen as he or she is and then forgiven can fully understand the gift of grace. For ourselves as well, this means the letting go of justification; of the desire to appear better than we are. If we do not let our God and others know us (not just know about us), we cannot know the wholeness and healing of forgiveness. And what we have not received we do not have to give to others.

There are reasons bridge-building and forgiveness are not popular and widely practiced, however. It can mean not only true detachment but also the sacrifice of everything, it can even mean the crucifixion of ourselves. It can, in actual practice, mean laying down our life for another or "for the many" as our Lord did. For those not ready to take on such forgiveness themselves, this can be very threatening. Paradoxically, the way of bridge-building, like the way of the Cross, can be a very lonely one at times on this earth. Christ built the only true and eternal bridge for mankind to heaven when he ascended the Cross, yet that was the time when He knew Himself most forsaken by both God and man.

Death was the only right way of reaching out to us and to the world, yet it was also the way of His leaving us and the world in the flesh. While others do not always see such a leave-taking as bridge-building, when leaving is an authentic response to God as was that of Jesus, it is indeed the most fully loving action possible. Jesus knew He belonged elsewhere and could continue to love those He was leaving only by going to the Father.

For us, the Church and its liturgical life are powerful tools in making forgiveness central to our lives. To be fully members of the Church, we must choose to make time to gather as the people of God; to "come out of the world" for definite periods. Making the choice to come faithfully for Sunday Divine Liturgy may be a real sacrifice for some; yet for the Orthodox Christian it is a necessary first step. As we are present at the liturgy, we bring our lives, ourselves, our loved ones, the whole world to offer in sacrifice—to make holy—before God. As we do this, we learn that the truest relationship we can have with others is to allow them to be themselves and to place them in God's hands. Liturgy teaches us that this is true prayer. It is the way of radically letting go rather than always attempting to control.

Christians, called into the priesthood of all believers as the Body of Christ offering the Liturgy on behalf of all and for all, become by that action the bridge between God and the world. This is a divine reality that transforms in time and eternity both those who participate and all they bring with them. We can forget this reality, for we remain ourselves, with our own personal boundaries and limitations, just as bread and wine remain bread and wine yet truly become the Body and Blood of Christ. To catch even a glimpse of this reality, however, is enough to know the God Who creates and sustains the whole universe at every instant of its being.

No one can prove this truth to another. It is something that can be proven only in the crucible of life's experience. Yet as we continue, our times of prayer will take on the force of reality and move beyond the hours of liturgy. We will continue to grow into God's own life and will learn how to bring ourselves, one another and the whole world before God as we go about our daily lives. We will eventually discover that the acceptance of boundaries and the building of bridges through the life-giving grace of forgiveness slowly replace our fallen approach to life. We will find ourselves on the road to heaven with those who have the eyes to see and the ears to hear, holding all others up to God in prayer.

A note on my sources for the comments on marriage:

I do not pretend to be a patristics scholar and I am sure that others will find better sources than I can quote. However, I do believe the source for much of the more negative approach to marriage can be traced to St. Gregory of Nyssa's treatise *On Virginity*. There is no question but that he is following some of the strands in St. Paul. However St. Paul himself is not so one-sided—in Ephesians he waxes very eloquent about the relationship between a man and wife and in 1 Corinthians he insists that a husband and wife "not refuse one another except *perhaps by agreement* for a season that you may devote yourselves to prayer; but then come together again, lest Satan tempt you by lack of self-control" (1 Cor 7.5). He also makes very clear when he is more negative about marriage that he is going by his own experience as a celibate and is aware that different people have different gifts. It is interesting to me that the above quotation from St. Paul is sometimes disregarded. I have known instances of couples whose marriages have nearly been broken up because one or the other spouse believes (and perhaps has even been told by a priest or monastic elder) that he or she is more spiritual than the other and therefore has the right to refuse the other *without agreement*. Rather than showing the love of Christ to one's spouse, this can become a tool of manipulation.

I do not question St. Gregory of Nyssa's sanctity, but the fact of the matter is that he is writing a polemical treatise on virginity, not on marriage. As I understand the Orthodox approach to life and theology, no one of the Fathers may be taken as infallible; all should be balanced with the Bible and the other writings of the Fathers.

If one has not read St. Gregory, and has read only (for example) St. John Chrysostom's *20th Homily On Ephesians*, one would come to quite a different conclusion. Here the love between a husband and wife is very blessed in and of itself. St. John is very clear that the children are beloved because of the love one has for the spouse: "And esteem her before all your friends, and above the children that are born of her, and let these very children be beloved by you for her sake." Today, of course, we have a scientific approach that would have been very foreign to the biblical and patristic writers. The question, for example, of a couple that have been told "scientifically" that they can never have children would not have come up, for who knew? Children are a miracle. Even today, some couples who have been told they cannot have children—or have even had operations to sterilize themselves—have gone on to conceive and bear children. So the teaching I have heard, that if a couple discovers that for biological reasons they are incapable of producing children, they should never sleep together, would not have come up earlier. Rather we have the Biblical examples of even elderly couples like Abraham and Sarah, Zachariah and Elizabeth, not to mention Joachim and Anna, who conceived against all hope in their old age, definitely according to the will of God.

Chapter Five

THE FULLNESS OF THE KINGDOM

*T*HIS TOPIC IS A CLASSIC one for Orthodox writers and speakers. I do not intend to say anything new on this subject; only to share my own thoughts and intuitions on a subject that is as vast as all eternity and that transcends all our rational concepts.

I want to qualify the phrase, "my own thoughts and intuitions." I believe one of the biggest road blocks for Christians today is our culture's paradoxical stance that "scientific" truth can and must be verified; we can and must have a single correct view about things (some would say everything) based on objective investigation, and that any truth that cannot fit into known scientific categories, especially a truth that cannot be weighed and measured, can only be a matter of opinion.

While scientific knowledge has opened up vistas our forebears could only have imagined, pushing our horizons far beyond local villages to the vast planet earth set in an even more vast solar system, which turns out to be just a tiny speck in the known physical universe, it seems that our culture's conception of God has shrunk proportionally. Major publications like *The New York Times*, *National Geographic*, and *Smithsonian* magazine imply through their manner of reporting that faith and theology—especially Christian faith and theology—are hopelessly anachronistic in our contemporary, post-modern and scientific world. Religion and religious events are reported as data displaying only the continuing irrationality and superstition plaguing that strange animal, *Homo sapiens.* These can be quite charming when found in an on-going primitive culture in some backwater such as the Amazon basin, but to many of our contemporaries, faith and theology are hopelessly out of place in anyone they would consider to be their intellectual peers.

I will always be grateful that some of my first reading as a teenager beginning my own search for faith in the 1950's was *Your God is Too Small,* a classic by the Anglican writer, J.B. Phillips, that is still in print.[1] The premise of this book has helped me enormously each time I have come across yet another "astounding" discovery or philosophy that is guaranteed to make Christian faith obsolete. Any god that can be destroyed is simply an idol, no matter how elaborately it may be constructed artistically, intellectually or psychologically.

When I was in high school, a teacher who organized a group for us teens used a simple illustration which has also stuck with me through the years. In a discussion of morals and ethics, he pointed out that fish who swim in the depths of the sea have lost the use of their eyes, and often have only vestigial ones, simply because they never use them. He said our conscience; our moral and spiritual senses were like that. We lose them if we don't use them.

I would submit that to approach our topic, *The Fullness of the Kingdom,* simply by thinking about it and describing it in words, will be an intellectual exercise of not much value. We can go down the list, quoting that wonderful passage in St. Paul's eighth chapter to the Romans: "The creation itself will be set free from its bondage to decay and obtain the glorious liberty of the children of God. We know that the whole creation has been groaning in travail together until now; and not only the creation, but we ourselves, who have the first fruits of the Spirit, groan inwardly as we wait for adoption as sons, the redemption of our bodies" (Rom 8.21–23). Not only we humans, but all of creation: every animal, plant, rock and stone—

[1] J.B. Phillips, *Your God is Too Small: A Guide for Believers and Skeptics Alike* (New York: Macmillan, 1953; paperback edition by Touchstone Press, 2004).

with the angels, principalities and powers—all will be present in this Kingdom.

And unless we see the Lord as simply a deluded prophet, since the Kingdom is not bound by time and space, we can say with Him "the Kingdom of heaven is at hand" (Mt 3.2). All of creation is present in the Kingdom now. The proclamation of the Kingdom which began His ministry is the proclamation of Emmanuel: God with us. Certainly there are intimations of this closeness in the Old Testament: In Deuteronomy we hear: "But the word is very near you; it is in your mouth and in your heart, so that you can do it" (Deut 30.14). And I believe St. Paul is saying the same thing in Christian terms when he says, "work out your own salvation with fear and trembling; for God is at work within you" (Phil 2.12–13).

Christians travel through the landscape of this Kingdom; it is the normal atmosphere we breathe on this earth. Yet if the God of many of us who call ourselves Christians is too small, our concept of the Kingdom of Heaven is nonexistent. In many areas, we have done well in taking to heart our Lord's words about the Last Judgment in St. Matthew's Gospel: I was hungry and you gave me food, I was thirsty and you gave me drink, I was a stranger and you welcomed me, I was naked and you clothed me, I was sick and you visited me, I was in prison and you came to me (Mt 25.35–36). Yet have we done this in such a way that those to whom we minister are left still hungering and thirsting, not learning that they can be satisfied only by the Bread of Life? (Jn 6.35). Have we left them clothed, but in garments that will not allow them to enter the Wedding Banquet or to put on the robe of incorruption by which the mortal is swallowed up by immortality? (Cf. Mt 22.11–14 and 2 Cor 5.4) Do they know that indeed, the Kingdom of heaven is at hand?

Humans have always observed things with their five senses and responded to the physical world they mediate. However, for the most part, at least until fairly modern times, they have also understood that there are other forms of knowledge. As Martin Buber points out in his classic book, *I and Thou*,[2] the knowledge gained in relationship to others is entirely different from that gained simply by knowing about them. Studying a rabbit by dissecting it is an entirely different thing from getting to know it as a pet. While in our culture we would call someone insane if they tried to get to know another person by physical dissection, most of us do spend quite a bit of time "dissecting" others, including God and His Kingdom, in words, rather than by knowing them through friendship and love.

All the talk, all the theology we may spout, will leave us with nothing but the corpse of our own dissected ideas about God and His Kingdom if we do not step out in love, faith, and prayer. Our God is a personal god; not simply a New Age Force. His Kingdom is love and truth. We can all too easily echo the words of Pilate who did not have the eyes to see or the ears to hear, when Truth stood right in front of him (Jn18.38).

But many of those around us will say that knowledge mediated through friendship and love is very unscientific. Not too long ago, I listened to two professional scientists in all seriousness scoffing at love and friendship as simply a delusion produced by chemical hormones and imbalance. The vision of blind fish swimming in the depths of the sea floated through my mind. These people were totally unaware of (or in denial about) spiritual senses that can mediate the experience of another; indeed mediate the experience of the entire universe, as surely as our physical senses mediate information about our physical environment.

In all fairness, some science is beginning to catch up with the fact that things ("subjects") are changed simply by being observed; that

[2]Martin Buber, *I and Thou* (New York: Charles Scribner's Sons, 1955).

there is and can be no such thing as a completely "objective" study or investigation.

In a fascinating, albeit controversial study of human consciousness first published in 1976 by the late Julian Jaynes, *The Origin of Human Consciousness in the Breakdown of the Bicameral Mind*, the author makes the case that all religion and belief in deity comes from nostalgia for our pre-conscious, bicameral past when humans could not differentiate between their outer sensory and inner psychological worlds. I truly enjoyed reading his book and think he may be accurate in his assessment of the origin of human consciousness, but I am unable to make the leap in logic that this therefore proves God does not exist, that Jesus was simply a person who attempted to reform Judaism by what "necessarily" became a "new religion for conscious men rather than bicameral men,"[3] and that there is no real content mediated by prayer, experience and intuition. Jaynes would go so far as to say that any experiences humans may believe they have of God are simply the result of a form of schizophrenic delusion; that the voices and visions which seem more real to the mystic than the external world are simply a matter of chemical imbalance or the result of a non-developed bicameral mind.

Why am I belaboring this point? I believe this sort of thinking is "in the air" today, and we are all influenced by it more than we realize. I would even say, as I have said many times before, that because of the media that most people are subjected to in this contemporary world, we are so brainwashed by this kind of thinking that we do not even know it. For those of you who enjoy the language of scholarship, a book by Alexei V. Nesteruk, *Light from the East*,[4] discusses

[3]Julian Jaynes, *The Origin of Consciousness in the Breakdown of the Bicameral Mind*, 2nd edition (Boston: Houghton Mifflin, 1990) 318–319.

[4]Alexei V. Nesteruk, *Light from the East: Theology, Science and the Eastern Orthodox Tradition* (Minneapolis: Augsburg Fortress Press, 2003).

with great erudition the long history of the relationship— or the ten-sion—between Christian faith and science. It is not an easy read, but I do recommend it for those who can plow through it. Nesteruk responds well to the assumption that faith is irrelevant to science or "real life."

Because of this "brainwashing," as I call it, I believe those of us living on the planet Earth today must work harder than those who went before us if we are to find ourselves in an environment con-ducive to love and faith, let alone prayer.

By "an environment conducive to prayer," however, I do not mean just seeking out some time in a Church or in an icon corner or a meditation room. The late Fr. Alexander Schmemann makes this point very clearly in his seminal book, *For the Life of the World*.[5] Speaking of the original sin, Father Alexander says "The sin was not that man neglected his religious duties. The sin was that he thought of God in terms of religion, i.e., opposing Him to life."[6]

What is our personal view of life? How do we approach the world? Do we see our surroundings and other people as things to be placed and controlled by us within the boundaries of what we con-sider to be "our life?" Do we think of religion as a way graciously to include God in our life and allow Him the courtesy of an occasional greeting? Is the Church just another one of the activities we sched-ule into our life to a greater or lesser degree?

Now I want literally to shift our focus. I'm sure many of you know that what can appear to be a factor of primitive art in Ortho-dox iconography is actually a very sophisticated approach called "inverse perspective." Even (or most especially) early iconographers were not "primitives." Inverse perspective places us within the gaze

[5]Revised edition. NY: Athens Printing Co., 1973 (Reprint edition available from St. Vladimir's Seminary Press, Crestwood, NY 10707)

[6]Ibid. p.18.

of the icon. It subconsciously challenges our perception that we are the center of the universe and can best perceive and judge reality from our own perspective.

Thus praying with icons can be a powerful tool in re-orienting our approach to life. Rather than sitting down to pray and placing the thought of God in our mind and imagination, as we stand before an icon we gradually begin to realize that it is the other way around: indeed we stand before God. By His gaze, He includes us in His Kingdom, the infinite universe He has created in time and space and redeemed by the Incarnation and Passion of Jesus for all eternity. As we allow ourselves to enter into His gaze, infinitesimally limited though our glimpse of it may be, we also allow ourselves to begin to see with the eye of our heart what cannot be seen by our five senses.

The Greek theologians had a word for this "sixth" or spiritual sense: they called it *nous*, a word to describe that faculty by which we know things not mediated by the five senses. In English we might say spiritual or intellectual understanding; intuition; the heart; prayer; experience; consciousness; awareness; even the much maligned term, "extra-sensory perception." Whatever we may call it, it is the way we enter into the life of another, experience things through his eyes, share his thoughts, or walk in his footsteps. Those who love understand this. Mothers often know when their children are in trouble—they don't need a phone call or a cry for help. If this is a biological sense, it is one that science has yet to categorize. Sometimes people know that a person has entered a crowded room, before seeing him or being told of his presence. If we can have this communication with other people, how much more does God have it with us, who are His children in the most intimate and fundamental sense?

This is communication without words—beyond words. Michael Gallatin speaks of this very eloquently in his book *Thirsting for God in a Land of Shallow Wells.*[7] This is heart speaking to heart; *nous* communication if you will. When we realize that God not only communicates with us in this way, but is the very ground of our being and the source of our life, we come to understand that any gaze we consider to be our own apart from His is sheer delusion. We cannot be on our own in God's Kingdom. The only way to be on our own or alone is to reject God so definitively that we accept our limited and warped view of reality in place of His. He will allow us to do this, and this is the classic definition of hell: a place where the fire of His love will eternally burn us as we choose eternally to reject it rather than allowing it to purify and hallow us.

Yet we need times of solitude and silence to recognize this—we must find time and space to recollect ourselves and to remind ourselves that we are in the presence of God and held by Him in eternity. Because our senses are so tuned to the clamor of this world, we must deny them at times the sights, sounds, smells, tastes and feelings that keep them stimulated, in order to cultivate our "sixth sense." Although He is God, in His humanity Jesus also needed time alone to pray with His Father in a world much quieter than ours. How much more do we need this as children of God, not by nature but by adoption?

God is He who has brought us into being, who allows us to stand here, and who surrounds us with His love. As much as His Kingdom is to come, it is here within us and among us. Let us long for it. Let us not allow the words He taught us to be vain and empty: "Your Kingdom come; Your will be done on earth as it is in heaven."

In whatever ways are possible for us, let us learn to pray that He may count us worthy to enter into the fullness of His Kingdom where for all eternity we shall rejoice with all of creation. Let us begin

[7]Ben Lomond, CA: Conciliar Press, 2002.

even now not only to be clothed by grace and fed with the immortal Bread of Life, but also in the bold words of St. Peter, to become partakers of the Divine Nature (2 Pet 1.4). May all that we do and speak here in this life be with the power and to the glory of Him Who lives forever with His Father and the Holy Spirit. Amen.

This paper was given at LaSalle University, Allentown, PA as part of the Campbell Lecture Series, March 2007. Used with permission.

Chapter Six

THE UNITY OF THE KINGDOM

I WANT TO BUILD on the concept of knowledge I introduced in my previous essay. I believe all attempts to approach Christian unity which rely on discussions of history, theology, and practice are doomed to failure. We've been there and done that. And as the saying goes, it is a form of insanity to keep doing the same things and expect to get different results. We could stay here 'till the cows come home, discussing and debating the relative merits of all the thousands of Christian or pseudo-Christian groups that exist here in America, let alone throughout the world. We Orthodox are not exempt from this condition of disunity, although we do tend to fight over things like whether we are Greek or Russian, whether women should have their hair covered in church and men should wear ponytails. We leave it to our Protestant brethren to debate whether it is necessary for a Christian to believe that Jesus is God; whether He really resurrected; whether there is a Trinity; whether the rite of Holy Communion is simply a memorial service or an actual participation in the Body and Blood of Christ, and (perhaps the most unmentionable topic of all) whether we can honor the Virgin Mary as the Mother of God, or *Theotokos*. Officially, while we would say that the Pope was the first Protestant, the Roman Catholics are with us on the above topics, but in some areas it seems the Roman Catholic Church is going through the Reformation all over again and some find themselves closer to Protestant groups than to the Orthodox Church.

I question, however, whether we Orthodox should pride ourselves on the pettiness of our divisions. The Lord said, "He who is faithful in a very little is faithful also in much; and he who is dishonest in a very little is dishonest also in much" (Lk 16.10). I can guarantee that there are non-Orthodox who stay away from us precisely because of our arrogance in proclaiming that we have the true faith while at the same time justifying our division into a multitude of ethnic jurisdictions. I know Episcopalians, or Anglicans as some now prefer to be called, who claim to be orthodox by virtue of being organized along similar ethnic lines.

Of course we Orthodox are also the last hold-outs to open communion and seemingly, therefore, the Christians least interested in the unity of Christ's Body on earth. If truth be told, there are Orthodox Christians who do absolutely refuse to dialogue with any non-Orthodox, and even have trouble sitting down to a friendly discussion with other members of their own jurisdiction who might believe differently about "ecumenism." I believe, however, it can be shown very easily that they are being non-traditional and acting in a non-"patristic" spirit that is contrary not only to Scripture but also to the fathers and mothers of the Church, beginning with St. Paul; going on through St. Justin the Martyr and St. Clement in the early Church; St. Basil, St. Macrina with the other "Cappadocians" who lived and taught during the fourth century; Ss Cosmas and Damian in the ninth century; St. Gregory Palamas in the fourteenth century; down closer to our own era with missionaries and teachers of the Church such as St. Herman of Alaska; Ss Innocent and Tikhon of Moscow and, for some of us, our contemporaries, Father Alexander Schmemann of Crestwood and Father Alexander Menn of Russia.

But let us continue a survey of the contemporary Christian scene. And I admit that I am not an unbiased observer here. From what I have read and observed, some Christian groups are based on the premise that, especially from the time of the fourth century, God abandoned His Church to the error and corruption which were cleaned up only in the sixteenth century by Martin Luther and the other "Reformers."[1] Other groups, including some Baptists, would claim that they are not Protestants; that there was a hidden or, to use an expression also favored by some traditionalist Orthodox, catacomb church that continued to believe and practice the pure faith during and after the fourth century when the arch-corruptor, St Constantine, declared Christianity to be the religion of the Roman Empire. As with Protestant groups, however, this pure religion could only be practiced freely and openly once the errors of Constantine's corruptions were revealed in the sixteenth century.

Then we have groups that teach very clearly that Jesus is not God while at the same time referring to themselves as Christian. Here we have the Jehovah's Witnesses, the last true Arians, who believe Jesus to be the Incarnate Word, the "first-born of creation," and who accept His pre-existence while denying His divinity. I'm sure I do not understand the teachings of the Mormons, but I think somehow they have a variation on this, although they as well as several other groups would claim that theirs is the only true faith. Any discussions I have had with Mormons have led me to believe that they, like the Seventh Day Adventists, see "teachings" more in terms of moral and ethical direction, including dietary prohibitions, rather than theology. While these groups believe Jesus is important, and use terminology borrowed from the classic Christian tradition, most deny both His divinity and belief in the Trinity. Some quasi-Hindu groups as well call themselves Christian and use Christian vocabulary such as "Christ" and "Incarnation" with meanings very different from almost all other Christian groups.

Does "the Unity of the Kingdom" mean that eventually we will all get it sorted out; that we all really believe in the same God, along with Jews, Moslems, Hindus and Buddhists; we just happen to be

[1]Cf. Matthew Gallatin, *Thirsting for God in a Land of Shallow Wells* (Ben Lomond, CA: Conciliar Press, 2002).i

comfortable with various forms of belief and practice? We even make jokes that up in heaven, God will have different rooms for each different group, and in all seriousness believe that is what Jesus meant when He said "In my Father's house are many mansions; if it were not so, would I have told you that I go to prepare a place for you?" (Jn 14.2).

With Jews and Moslems, we do believe that God is One. It can be demonstrably argued that the genius of Mohammed was to take what he saw as the best of Judaism and Christianity and create a synthesis that he felt would be acceptable to his people. There is no question that he succeeded in this. It can even be demonstrably argued, given the influence of Islam in Europe in the late Middle Ages, that the *Sola Scriptura* of western Christians during and after the time of the Reformation owes something to Mohammed's insistence that his text be taken as infallible. He could not appeal to a living body of tradition; his claim was that he wrote the Koran under direct divine inspiration, in the same way that some Christian groups seem to claim the Biblical writers wrote the Old and New Testaments. I could continue, but I think that is enough analysis of the present situation of "communities of faith."

Perhaps not everyone is familiar with a mythical story told of Alexander the Great. One of the kings of Gordion (the capital of Phrygia in central Anatolia, modern Turkey, from 1100–200 B.C.), dedicated his chariot to Zeus who allegedly helped him tie the yoke to the pole in an intricate knot. The king declared that whoever could untie this knot would become the ruler of the world. Many wise men, many rulers came, studied it, puzzled over it, and tried to unravel it, but all in vain. In 334 B.C., young Alexander came to Gordion. He took one look at the knot and unraveled it with one stroke of his sword. Then it is said that he turned and proclaimed, "Thus do I unravel all Gordion Knots," and went on to conquer the world.

For some reason the situation of Christendom reminds me of the Gordion Knot. " . . . the word of God is living and active, sharper than any two-edged sword, piercing to the division of soul and spirit, of joints and marrow, and discerning the thoughts and intentions of the heart," says the apostle to the Hebrews (4.12). Jesus Christ, the Word of God, our Lord God and Savior, is alive and well, and very capable of taking on any and all Gordion Knots. But many Christians don't seem to believe that. Efforts at unity seem more to involve holding conferences, workshops, referendums—the equivalent of sitting down, like the wise men and rulers of our story, attempting to unravel our tangled situation by human wisdom, study, and efforts. We need the Unity of the Kingdom, not our own plans of merger. We do not own parts of the Body of Christ like companies we can modify and dispose of by majority vote or takeover, hostile or otherwise.

It comes down, I think, to the very simple question Jesus asked His disciples in Palestine all those long years ago. "But who do you say that I am?" (Mt 16.15). How many manifestos, volumes of theology, and articles of faith have been written and published in various human attempts to answer that question? It is the question He asks of us still, and as the Father answers through us, we find the unity of His Holy Spirit in His eternal Kingdom. All the answers that have not led us to this unity come from "flesh and blood" (Mt 16.17).

If we believe in a living, personal God Who is in total charge of the created universe, whose Spirit can guide us and lead us into all truth (Jn 16.13), we will be willing to wait upon Him. We will understand that as long as our attempts at unity are attempts to create a humanly strong, powerful Christian Body, we will fail. He will continue to humble us by our divisions until we come to see with St. Paul that the power of God is made perfect in human weakness (2 Cor 12.9). "The foolishness of God is wiser than men, and the weakness of God is stronger than men" (1 Cor 1.25). Look how arrogant we can be even in our pitifully divided state! If by some *tour de force* we were able to wave the equivalent of a magic wand and wake up with all the present groups who claim to be Christian unified into one large organization, I believe that the result would be horribly demonic. We are no better than those who went before us and we have the technology to wreak far greater devastation than they. If they could not resist the temptations to sponsor inquisitions, witch hunts, pogroms—all in the name of Christ—I shudder to think what we could and would do. We are very capable of losing the vision of our eyes that allows us to see the difference between right and wrong. It seems to me there are very clear examples of this. One which comes to my mind and lies heavy on my heart is based on the experiences I have had with Christians who protest torture in the killing of lobsters for food, but who do not bat an eye at the torture and dismembering of a human infant with obviously well-developed senses, an infant that under other circumstances would have received the best of care in a clinic for premature births. We may shudder at archaeological findings of mass graveyards of infants killed at birth or shortly thereafter in sacrifices to the gods of early nations, but those infants had a prayer said over their remains; they were not tossed out as garbage. Dare we say that we are better in our days?

Yes, in the midst of this tangled, sinful, human situation, we do well to be humble. Let us be strong in the Lord, but for His glory, not for our own sakes. We need to be sure that we are grounded and rooted in Him; that we grow into the Eucharistic life He gives us as Christians. As it says in the book of Revelation, we are to give thanks and glory to Him who loves us and has freed us from our sins by His blood and has made us a kingdom, priests to His God and Father (Rev 1.5–6), priests to serve on behalf of all mankind and all of creation. As priests, we are called first to offer sacrifice for ourselves (Heb 7.27), then to raise up to God that part of creation which has been given into our stewardship. Further, we are not to bow down or enslave ourselves to things which have no life in themselves, whether they be gods of the intellect, money, or art, or demons of pride, gluttony, lust, or anger.

Let us seek soundness for our eyes (Mt 6.2) so that we may see creation, others, and the world around us as windows through which the glory of God shines. "To the pure, all things are pure; to the corrupt, all things are corrupt" (Ps 18.26; Titus 1.16). The whole of creation is given life by God and created good (Gen 1.31), capable of redemption and of proclaiming His glory, and is not meant to be co-opted by fallen creatures for their own twisted agendas.

Einstein is quoted as saying: "For some people there are no miracles. For others, all of life is a miracle." May we learn to say with the Psalmists, "How manifold are Your works, O Lord! In wisdom have You made them all!" (Ps 104.24). "The heavens declare the glory of God and the firmament proclaims His handiwork!" (Ps 19.1).

If we can see God present in and through His creation, in the smallest particle of energy making up the smallest part of an atom on earth, as well as in the furthest reaches of space, we can also come to see Him present in the bread and wine of Communion. Christ's sacrifice of Himself on behalf of all mankind and all creation is eternally present to us whether or not we choose to enter into that reality. If His death and sacrifice seem too far away to be meaningful to us, then perhaps our hearts will be stirred by those Christians in our own lifetime who have suffered and continue to suffer for the sake of Christ. The Church produced far more martyrs in the twentieth century than under three centuries of persecutions under the Roman Empire. There are all-too-frequent bulletins from Kosovo, Palestine, Indonesia, China, North Korea, not to mention the streets of our own cities, asking prayers for those who are suffering, being persecuted and killed for the sake of truth and righteousness. May we not take their sacrifice lightly. Christ did not die on the cross, and these people, including infants, are not being tortured and maimed, living and dying in such conditions, so that we can organize church trips to the nearest Casino. Rather let us ask to be counted worthy of becoming disciples of Christ, of taking up our Cross daily and following Him (Lk 9.23). May we learn to say with St. Paul, "Now I rejoice in my sufferings for your sake, and in my flesh I complete what is lacking in Christ's afflictions for the sake of his body, that is, the church" (Col 1.24). If enslaved by the passions of this life (Rom 6.6), we do not have the freedom to take on such suffering, let us at least take up the cross and suffering of fighting against these same passions, calling on the redeeming Passion of Christ.

We Orthodox say that the bread and cup of Communion consummate our commitment, our marriage with the Lamb, in His Body which is the Church just as we would say that the marriage bed consummates the commitment already made between a man and a woman, rather than being something that is tried out ahead of time to see if it will work. We do not condemn those outside the Orthodox Church who have other practices, nor, for example, do we refrain from communion at a Protestant service because we do not believe that Christ is present. He is present everywhere and fills all things. We acknowledge, rather, the differences that exist in belief and practice; that while we recognize the real presence of Christ in the Eucharist, others will receive the cup with a very different vision.

Recognizing that unity of faith, love and practice does not exist here does not lessen our commitment, indeed our obligation, to pray that God's Kingdom come and His will be done on earth as it is in heaven. Let us all indeed pray to God that even in our days He will count us worthy to be found in His eternal Kingdom. There, where all creation shares in the life and the vision of God, may we find ourselves and one another in the Unity of the Spirit and the bond of peace which He alone gives together with His only begotten Son, our Lord God and Savior Jesus Christ. Amen.

This paper was given at LaSalle University, Allentown, Pennsylvania, as part of the Campbell Lecture Series, March 2007. Used with permission.

Chapter Seven

MONASTICISM AND THE WAY
OF RADICAL PEACE

I WOULD SUBMIT THAT on this earth, peace is not an end in itself. We do not believe in an earthly utopia—there will be disagreements, violence, terrorism and wars until the end of time, for the prince of this world is still allowed to be active. Rather than seeking peace, I think that, as Orthodox Christians, we are meant to seek the Lord first, and then He gives His peace to fill our lives.

In my own experience as a monastic, I find that there are several levels we have to deal with if we are going to find peace. I have heard monastics from other communities echo our own experience—in the middle of a time of incredible struggle and tension, with sisters at odds with each other and everything seeming to go wrong, visitors will arrive for a few hours or days and leave with the remark that they have found the monastery "so peaceful." Of course in some instances, this may be because the sisters have learned to behave nicely no matter what emotions and thoughts they may be hiding, but I believe it is something more than that. One of the great joys and inspirations of monastic life is to be living with people of enormous good will who truly want to be all that God wants them to be. It is amazing how such good-willed people can still offend each other, but we certainly do. If one perseveres in this life, one soon learns the sometimes bizarre lengths the devil and his minions will go to in order to cause divisions and strife in the monastery.

The "secret," if there is one to surviving in this environment, is never to forget that the others are good-willed and that each person is loving and striving to the utmost. Many of the monastic writers say that we should always consider others to be better than ourselves and I have found this to be very practical advice. If each woman remembers that if she faces the struggle with the demons within herself without getting side-tracked by obsessing on what others should be like or should or should not be doing, then peace can and does reign.

This does not mean pretending hurtful behaviors and words have not been witnessed; it does mean not judging other's motives and not holding on to grudges. It means forgiving one another from the heart "seventy times seven" each day and being willing to accept that same forgiveness for ourselves while realizing that we may be mistaken in our assessment of others and of situations.

As Orthodox Christians, and please God, that is what a monastic is first and foremost, we are called to spiritual warfare with all the weapons God has given us in the Church. As we persevere in this life of warfare, giving up all physical weapons of violence, we discover other levels of violence within ourselves. We do not need bombs, guns, or missiles in order to kill. As each of us faces the venom within ourselves that slips out either intentionally or unintentionally in sullen looks, resentful words, and hurtful actions, we may sometimes feel that the physical warfare of others may be less harmful in the eternal scheme of things. Yet no one, with the exception of the Lord Himself and His blessed Mother, has been free from this kind of sin.

I would say from my own experience that some of the angriest people I have met (and at one point I would definitely have included myself in that category) are unable to see their own anger. They become furious at the mere suggestion that they might be angry! They see themselves as very nice people – or at least as justified in their anger. We see this often in places like monasteries – people who have not faced their anger finding themselves stripped of their usual comforts and self-willed ways of doing things, can begin to act out— sometimes even in physically violent ways. But because they cannot take responsibility for their own anger, they will blame the monastery: I'm such a good, nice person. This monastery and these sisters or this particular sister must be evil (or today probably the word would be "sick") because they are forcing me to act this way.

No one can force us to act out in anger. It is our own response, more or less conscious, depending on how responsible we are for our lives.

For most of us, it takes years and years before we can become fully responsible; able and willing to say: "Yes, I was angry; I did say (or do) that; I did mean to hurt that person; I'm sorry; please forgive me." Even when we believe that the other person meant to hurt us first. As we become like Christ, we come to see that retaliation is not the answer. Humanly speaking, we cannot rise above such hurts, but when we admit our powerlessness and are willing to accept the grace of Christ and grow beyond our fallen nature into His divine nature, then we also can say: "Father, forgive them." Even when they themselves may not want or ask for that forgiveness, we forgive—not to get the final moral victory over our opponent, but in order to make room for the Lord and His peace in our hearts. We have to do this. We have to be willing radically to let go of others so they also can fall into the hands of the living God. How often do our best efforts to fix others and situations result rather in substituting our own fallen and limited solutions for the power of our all-powerful God?

This willingness to let go in love and forgiveness is the real power of martyrdom and the reason why monasticism has been called at times the way of "White martyrdom." We give up ourselves completely, trusting that God will be able to act through us even by—or perhaps most especially by—our death, or the death of our cherished dreams. Any other motive for martyrdom, the kind born of hatred, desire for justification or revenge, for example, simply adds to the escalating violence—as we see so clearly in the Middle East now.

When we haven't dealt with the roots of our anger, while we may be able to put a lid on it in certain situations, it will sit there building up steam to explode through another vent when we aren't looking. Thus the phenomenon of the loving husband and father who is a vicious boss—or the other way around: Someone who is absolutely charming at work or in church or other outside social settings, but is transformed into a monster by walking through the front door at home. I've heard stories from children of well-respected professionals such as doctors, and even clergy, of their cowering in the closets until they knew what mood mommy or daddy would be in when they came home.

Once we have admitted our own inner anger and violence, we must pray and use every means the Lord puts at our disposal to come to terms with it. The disciplines of the monastic life aim at helping us to cut out this kind of anger. We have the opportunity to pray daily; to hear in the services the stories of others who have conquered through love and forgiveness; to be fed by the Lord's own life of love and forgiveness through the Eucharist; to admit to our own sins and failings and receive the healing of confession, and to read books by the saints as well as by contemporary professionals, which can help us to understand where our own anger is coming from and how best to cut it out by the roots. And perhaps even more importantly, we have the opportunity to live very closely with other women whom we did not choose for any romantic association—strong women from many very different backgrounds. This is the arena where we learn to fight by using our anger rightly, against the thoughts and feelings that threaten to destroy us from within with a death far more deadly than any lion in the coliseum.

Looking beyond this arena of our daily life, today especially we are confronted with a world seemingly driven by anger. While it is true that many of us would hope our country would always be pure and holy and acting from Orthodox Christian principles, we need to face the fact that this did not happen even under the holy emperors of Byzantium and Moscow.

If we as Orthodox Christians cannot have unity of heart, soul and mind, how can we be surprised at, or judge others who do not have the spiritual riches given to us for our salvation in the Church? The Lord said: "But I say to you that every one who is angry with his brother shall be liable to judgment; whoever insults his brother shall be liable to the council, and whoever says, 'You fool!' shall be liable to the hell of fire" (Mt 5.22). I would submit that it is a far greater sin for Orthodox in America to engage in party spirit, whether it be on the level of American Democratic-Republican party politics or ethnic-jurisdictional differences or within jurisdictions, which seminary or monastery is "more truly orthodox" than it is for Jewish Israelis and Moslem Arabs to be killing one another with external weapons of violence. " . . . he who did not know, and did what deserved a beating, shall receive a light beating. Every one to whom much is given, of him will much be required; and of him to whom men commit much they will demand the more" (Lk 12.48).

The only "label" I want to wear is that of an Orthodox Christian monastic. I will not try to define myself otherwise. For this reason, my approach to this topic has been to look to Jesus Christ as the only Way to both true monasticism and true, radical peace.

The more we try to sustain our own ideas about things, including what it means to be a monastic as well as a pacifist apart from God's reality, the less our attempts to grow into His calling for us and to live with the peace that only He can give will be blessed with His providential empowerment.

I found that the Revised Standard Version of the Bible lists 426 references to the word "peace," beginning with Genesis 15.15 "As for yourself (referring to Patriarch Abraham), you shall go to your fathers in peace; you shall be buried in a good old age" and ending with Revelation 6:4 "And out came another horse, bright red; its rider was permitted to take peace from the earth, so that men should slay one another; and he was given a great sword."

I was struck by these "bookend" references. The first suggests the nice, almost cozy type of peace our world would seem prefer: To quote the Litany of Supplication: "That we may complete the remaining time of our life in peace and repentance," finding a "painless, blameless and peaceful" ending to our life. And without this type of peace at least for some people, for some of the time in some places, life on this planet earth would be unbearable.

The second reference from Revelation gives us the other picture we face all too often in our world: God has permitted peace to be taken from the earth that men should slay one another. This is the other side of the reality we live with and if it is all that we live with, we can be driven to despair and insanity.

The literary genre begun by Tolkein's Ring Trilogy is so immensely appealing to people, I believe, because it plays on these two contrasting themes. The hero (or band of heroes) is called to go on an epic, often super-human quest through incredible dangers, treachery, violence, warfare and ultimate tests of strength, intelligence, and endurance. And this quest is necessarily interspersed with interludes of comforting peace. The word peace, of course, comes from the Latin word, pax, whose root is pacisi, to agree. There is a world of difference between real unity and peace and superficial agreements. Without friends and supporters who in some way agree with us, with whom we share a unity of mind and soul, we can begin to doubt our sanity. Those who find themselves surrounded by constant doubt and disagreement can persevere, but only through a strong, living relationship with the Lord Who is the source of all unity, agreement and therefore, peace.

I would submit that any peace, to be a true peace, must be literally comforting. We have lost the root meaning of the word in our common speech. It comes from the Latin word, *fortis*, meaning "strength", modified with the prefix *com*, meaning "together", we understand that at their best, times of peace and comfort are meant to give us the strength and courage we need to return to our God-given, demanding tasks. "Comfort, comfort my people, says the Lord," in the prophecy of Isaiah. Yet for us, (and here is where I think we can see the danger of trying to set up definitions apart from God's reality) comfort has degenerated to visions of soft pillows and blankets, easy chairs and walking shoes that may indeed help us to find necessary relaxation, yet may also tempt us away from our higher calling and enervate us rather than strengthen us.

I think this is the difficulty with some approaches to pacifism. If peace for someone means being unendingly comfortable, in the common usage of that word, then I believe that person has misunderstood the nature of peace. And I believe a peace based on this assumption will not be able to stand.

From a search for "Peace" in sayings of the Lord in the Gospels:

"And if the house is worthy, let your peace come upon it; but if it is not worthy, let your peace return to you" (Mt 10.13).

"Do not think that I have come to bring peace on earth; I have not come to bring peace, but a sword" (Mt 10.34). "Do you think that I have come to give peace on earth? No, I tell you, but rather division . . . " (Lk 12.51).

"And he awoke and rebuked the wind, and said to the sea, "Peace! Be still!" And the wind ceased, and there was a great calm" (Mk 4.39).

"Have salt in yourselves, and be at peace with one another" (Mk 9.50).

"When a strong man, fully armed, guards his own palace, his goods are in peace . . . " (Lk 11.21).

"Whoever does not bear his own cross and come after me, cannot be my disciple. For . . . what king, going to encounter another king in war, will not sit down first and take counsel whether he is able with ten thousand to meet him who comes against him with twenty thousand? And if not, while the other is yet a great way off, he sends an embassy and asks terms of peace. So therefore, whoever of you does not renounce all that he has cannot be my disciple (Lk 14. 27, 31–33).

"As he was now drawing near, at the descent of the Mount of Olives, the whole multitude of the disciples began to rejoice and praise God with a loud voice for all the mighty works that they had seen, saying, 'Blessed is the King who comes in the name of the Lord! Peace in heaven and glory in the highest!' And some of the Pharisees in the multitude said to him, 'Teacher, rebuke your disciples.' He answered, 'I tell you, if these were silent, the very stones would cry out.' And when he drew near and saw the city he wept over it, saying, 'Would that even today you knew the things that make for peace! But now they are hid from your eyes. For the days shall come upon you, when your enemies will cast up a bank about you and surround you, and hem you in on every side, and dash you to the ground, you and your children within you, and they will not leave one stone upon another in you; because you did not know the time of your visitation'" (Lk 19.37–44).

"Peace I leave with you; my peace I give to you; not as the world gives do I give to you. Let not your hearts be troubled, neither let them be afraid" (Jn 14.27).

"I have said this to you, that in me you may have peace. In the world you have tribulation; but be of good cheer, I have overcome the world" (Jn 16.33).

Chapter Eight

WORTH AND WORSHIP

*I*T IS NO SECRET THAT the Orthodox Church has a full and rich tradition of prayer and worship, writings and scripture, asceticism and celebration. In fact, many of those outside the Church can see us as a bit "over done." Why do we need all those books? Why do we need all those saints and icons? Why so many long services with so much singing and repetition? Why spend at least half of every year fasting and then, for example, go on to celebrate for twelve full days of Christmas, long past the point when everyone else has thrown away their tree and gotten back to "work as usual?" Why do some parishes still insist that people put on their best clothes to come to church? Wouldn't it be easier and feel more "natural" to simplify things?

These are not questions I've made up to write this essay. They are questions we hear many times at our monastery, even sometimes from those who are officially in the Orthodox Church.

And indeed, it seems that even some parts of the Orthodox Church are moving in this direction. A number of faithful seem to be unaware that there is a full Orthodox tradition of teaching, including books beginning with the Holy Bible, to help them learn to pray and to understand their faith and their Church. They forget that the saints are very much alive in Christ and part of daily life, with icons mediating their presence much as family photographs keep loved ones before us. They can become uncomfortable or bored with long services filled with singing and chanting, not understanding that they are the best antidote to all of the media bombarding them from every direction with constantly repeated messages of materialism, consumerism and lust. Many have never been encouraged to attempt to fast and so see no need for this God-given means for self-control and acceptance of who we are in relationship to Him; the best way to acceptance of humility. Without experiencing fasting, they don't know that it also helps us appreciate the great celebrations of His creation, redemption and gifts to us, putting them in the perspective of His life rather than our own fallen ways of celebration. They can seem to forget the enormity of His great love and generosity towards us. Remembering Him with even a little understanding of Who He is and what He is doing for us, leads us in turn to want to give Him our best, which certainly can including dressing up and putting our best foot forward when we enter His house.

No doubt each of these issues could become the subject of an essay, but I want to write about the common thread that I see underlying all of them.

Unwittingly changed by the technology that surrounds us, most of us have lost the "antennae" to be attuned to any reality other than the immediate, material world we can see, hear, touch and smell. We are a generation for whom "faith has grown cold" (cf. Lk 18.8). The vision of God and the glory of His Kingdom are primarily nice ideas that we may think about from time to time, especially when going to Church, but they are hardly the realities that shape our daily lives.

Without a living relationship with the God Who has revealed Himself to us and Who made us in His own image, we find ourselves creating our own gods, intellectual and otherwise, formed by our own ideas of who or what such a god should be. As the old proverb goes, we create him, her or it in our own image. And we lose the power of the creative Spirit of God, the Father of our Lord Jesus Christ in our lives, Who leads us on into an eternity of growth into the fullness of His divine life.

Without the ability to see and remember the house of our true Father in heaven from which all of us have strayed, if we do manage to "come to ourselves" in the pigpen of our lives (Lk 15.11–12), we have virtually no incentive to leave it. Rather than formulating plans to return to our Father's house, and perhaps persuade others to come with us, we try to figure out how best to survive in the pigpen, as a friend of mine put it. We even find that others are already helping us to stay put: "Why change? You are beautiful as you are. Idolatry, fornication and promiscuity, false witness, gluttony, addiction, covetousness and similar life-styles are all that you can manage in the pigpen, so we will help you lose all feelings of guilt and anxiety over them."

There are many drawbacks to this approach, of course. The most obvious being that the nature of our humanity created in fact in God's image and likeness is, as St. Augustine put it, restless until it finds its rest in Him.[1] While we may have lost the conscious awareness of our origin, God's reality is imprinted in our DNA and fills the atmosphere of the created universe we move in. He will not force us to turn to Him, but He will hold out the invitation to do so as long as we live. We can do our best to smother that spark within us, but we can never completely extinguish it.

When we do try to smother that spark, in ourselves or in others, we kill as well our innate sense of worth. Created to be worthy of the Kingdom of God, of His great love for us and the eternal, infinite outpouring of His gifts, we (and others) try to organize our lives into a size and shape we feel we can control completely. We harden ourselves into small, twisted and damaged vessels, incapable of receiving more than the most elementary gift of existence.

Yet because the reality is that we are not and can never be in control of the universe, we also can never completely get away from God. If we have totally convinced ourselves consciously that our self-created reality is all that exists, our subconscious will be constantly

[1] *The Confessions of St. Augustine*, Book I, Chapter 1.e

bombarded with evidence to the contrary. Part of us will always know that we are supposed to be bigger, more loving, joyful and giving, more attuned to the needs of others and less centered on our own fallen selves.

This subconscious understanding, forced to compare itself with what we have made of our lives, will lead to a subtle and increasingly pervasive sense of lack of self-worth. I believe that our entire society is riddled with this lack of self-worth. While children are born knowing they are worth something, few can grow up in our fallen world without this sense of worth being replaced by a sense of shame, wrongful guilt and despair. I think this is the obvious reason that suicide is the leading cause of death among teen-agers and young adults.

Yet even if it were somehow possible to have grown up with parents, siblings, friends and educators who surrounded us with love and support, we cannot help but hear the constant message from advertisers that we are not really good enough—unless we buy this particular shampoo, use that credit card, drive a particularly attractive vehicle, vacation in spots most revered by consumerism, or whatever else is being pushed. Even churches can buy in to this form of advertising. This is a very ancient message, used first by the Snake: " . . . when you eat of this fruit . . . " (Gen 2.17). While we may think we can ignore these messages, today especially, with the added force of the technology-driven media that can surround us from the moment our alarms go off in the morning till we fall asleep in front of the television at night, they creep into our subconscious, waging a continuous war against our innate common sense.

How many of us can look at our face in a mirror and tell ourselves we are worthy of God's creation; worthy of His great gifts of love, redemption and salvation? It is an interesting and good exercise to try, and to repeat if we find it difficult.

However, let us not be tempted by the contemporary fad of "affirmations" that suggest we tell ourselves we are worthy on our own, somehow apart from God, of material wealth, power over others, and all the other "values" the world, the flesh and the devil have always held out to fallen human beings. Nevertheless, let us learn to recognize, rejoice in and give thanks to God for all the gifts He does give us, understanding always that they are from Him, of His making and given to us in stewardship to be shared with others and returned to Him with interest (Mt 25.14–30).

To begin to counteract the message of worthlessness our fallen world has given and continues to give us, we have to work hard to regain our awareness of God; to gain the vision of His worth so that we may understand our own worth, created as we are in His image. We need to turn to Him and, by daily practice, regain the ability to hear His word spoken to us in personal and liturgical prayer, reading and the providence of our daily lives. We need to enter into His worship, offering Him the honor, reverence, prayer, thanksgiving and even adoration, which are uniquely due to Him. The more we enter in to this worship (a word which means simply giving Him His due: His "worthship"), the more we will consciously and unconsciously be able to see our own worth.

And we need to ask ourselves how then we can best offer Him the worship that is His due? What is our best? For example, I question if something isn't wrong when people literally cannot be comfortable wearing anything but glorified pajamas, even standing before God in formal worship. Is that really the only self-image they have? Would they be willing to meet the President of the United States at a banquet dressed like that? Would they choose to stay away from the banquet because they would rather not put on their wedding garment? (cf. Mt 22.1–14). Or if they do put on their "best," not seeing themselves as people innately beautiful, made attractive by

God, will they dress rather to attract attention, lust and envy from others?

The list goes on: People who uncritically accept a drab, dingy and shabby church building for the worship of God, may have a problem living in anything but spacious and beautiful homes themselves. Choir members who see no need to practice and at best struggle to stay on pitch during services may be offended when listening to a musical concert or recording that is not up to "their standards." Some of those who contend that modern people are not capable of standing with attention before God through long services may be found standing for hours in long lines waiting for tickets to a special event—and on it goes.

As we erode our sense of what is due to God, while we may seem to maintain our standards of self-worth, we are really setting ourselves up for the ultimate loss of our real worth, our faith, our parishes, churches and our humanity. Those of us who are concerned to see that our children have left the faith may need look no further for the cause.

Humanly, many of us may well continue to find ourselves in situations where we see no hope; no value or worth to our lives and even to our faith and our parishes. Let us learn to turn to God Who alone can and does show us our very great worth. Let us encourage one another to worship in truth and in love the One Who loved and valued each of us enough to die for us, returning us with His Own risen and ascended Humanity to the House of His Father in Heaven.

Chapter Nine

STABILITY

*R*ECENTLY WE WERE invited to join friends in a nearby parish who were celebrating their sixty-fifth wedding anniversary. The testimonial dinner was inspiring. Not only have these two people been married for 65 years, but they met in this same parish as children and lived out their lives and raised their children there. Other couples from the parish spoke of the inspiration these two have been. They saw their struggles and saw that it was very difficult at times for them to overcome obstacles to loving each other and staying together. Yet they did it, rooted and grounded in Christ and, as their son said, it is truly an honor and an inspiration to see these two people who still love each other very much. Young, newly-married couples also spoke of the influence these two had on their decisions to marry and stay in the Church.

Such an example of stability is rare in our world today. While it has always been the basis for serious spiritual endeavor—Saint Isaac the Syrian and St. John Climacus along with many other monastic saints place it at the heart of the monastic life—such stability is rare even in our monasteries today, peopled with men and women who come from our very mobile culture.

The need to find work and support a family explains much of the moving that families and individuals do today. Nevertheless, the compulsion to "move on" even when such necessity does not exist is endemic to our culture. I would like to explore both the positive asceticism of stability and the roots of this instability. I believe we need to take these seriously if we are going to grow into our full stature, rooted and grounded in Christ.

The Christian ascetic life has always been an attempt on our part to return to the life of Paradise as fully as God's grace on this fallen earth allows. Along with abstaining from meat, for example, monastics are counseled to stay within their monastery as within the Garden of Eden, not wandering as Adam and Eve did when cast out from God's presence (Gen 3), learning through the practice of obedience to listen to His voice rather than to those of the snakes they meet and "working with their own hands" (1 Thess 4.11) as Adam tended the garden. Along with this, as much as any married couple, they are to learn in practical ways to love all they meet as Christ, beginning with those they are to live with in community for the rest of their lives.

In contrast to this, friends tell us that in the world today if one stays on at a job for longer than two years, one is not commended for stability but thought to be "stagnating." Within the contemporary Church, our parish clergy are often caught in this trap as well, either moving or being moved on arbitrary timetables. In a marriage, when a spouse goes through a difficult patch and seems not to be his or her usual loving self, many are told that the right and immediate course of action is to get out of such a difficult relationship. In this thinking, "comfort zones" are non-negotiable and people should move on before the problems build up and become intolerable.

It is true that we should take responsibility for ourselves and remove ourselves from situations that we know to be abusive and, thereby, not lead others into sin and temptation. As adults, we can be honest victims the first time someone is abusive. After that, if we knowingly choose to remain in that same situation, we are willing accomplices, or to use "twelve-step" language, "enablers." Nevertheless, what may be considered as abuse today is pretty questionable. Some seem to feel people are being abused if they are asked simply to "bear another's burden," not to take offence at words, glances or gestures, or to put aside their own desires and agendas for a time so that another can have the basic necessities of life.

We cannot accept such definitions of abuse for ourselves and follow the Gospel. When families, churches and monasteries accept such standards, they too are no longer living Christ's Gospel. We should draw boundaries about tolerating such behavior. Even children are not served well by being allowed to believe that their bad behavior is tolerated. They instinctively know they are loved truly when their families, parishes, schools and friends call out the best that is in them. "Tough love" is not an unattainable ideal but God's own way of loving in the very real world He has created.

However, when we are bothered by adults behaving immaturely and refusing to accept the sometimes harsh realities of life, judging them is not the answer—for the obvious reason that often the sins and failures that bother us most in others are the besetting sins that we are not willing to face in ourselves (cf. Mt 7.3–5). Indeed, when we have come to terms with our own sinfulness, rather than judging, we find ourselves with compassion for others who likewise struggle with their own sinfulness. When we struggle with and/or leave a relationship, a family, a parish, a monastery, a group of friends or a job because we find ourselves able only to see the sins and failures in all around us, it is a great grace if eventually we come to see rather that as the famous cartoon figure, Pogo, put it: "We have met the enemy and he is us." Part of the instability of our times is directly traceable to our running away from ourselves. It is increasingly obvious that people move around today, as a friend of mine put it, "plugged into everything and everyone but themselves." She continued, "And you know, if you run away, wherever you go, there you are."

Let us look at this same phenomenon from another perspective. Psalm 91 is chanted daily in monasteries: "A thousand may fall at your side, ten thousand at your right hand; but it will not come near you."

How can this be true? The Psalm continues: "Because you have made the Lord your refuge, the Most High your habitation, no evil shall befall you, no scourge come near your tent" (Ps 91.7, 10). The key here is to make the Lord our refuge, the Most High our habitation. Elsewhere the Psalms tell us: "Put not your trust in princes, in sons of men, in whom there is no salvation" (Ps 146.3). If we trust in ourselves, in those around us, in our situation, in anyone or anything other than God, we will be disappointed. Our spouse, our children, our siblings, our fellows in community or at work, our friends and companions, even our careers and the places we live will never be able to live up to our expectations if we want them to replace God in our lives. As we know so well these days, the very earth we consider to be solid beneath us and the skies above us can become violent and destructive. Nor can we fill this role of salvation for others. Any of us may choose deliberately to betray or disappoint others in this fallen world. Far more often, however, we are simply being true to what we see and understand as limited and finite human beings, not capable of knowing, let alone fulfilling the expectations others have for us.

If we enter a monastery, become part of a parish, choose a career or the way of marriage and family for reasons other than the belief that ultimately we belong to God and that as we stand before Him in prayer this is the possibility He is holding out for us, we can be sure that all of those other reasons will ultimately fail us. The Lord will use "tough love" and allow us to face the consequences of our fallen choices. Our spouse may turn out to be a philandering addict, the technology we have learned for our job may become obsolete, the old ladies (or the converts) in our parish may insist on holding on to some very un-Orthodox traditions, our children may grow up to be ungrateful criminals, we may come to see that our monastery is not filled with clairvoyant, shining lights . . . And we will feel hurt, betrayed and angry.

But if in our hurt we will finally turn to God, He is able to use every mistake we have ever made to bring us to the fullness of the Kingdom of Heaven. Even when we have taken His gift of life and tried to remake it according to our own plan, warping it, stunting it compared with the fullness He originally held out for us, we have not hurt Him. Nor does the hurt we have done to ourselves by our behavior, words, and actions limit His power to save. St. Paul, who knew the depths of his own betrayal of the Lord was able to proclaim confidently in the powerful eighth chapter of his letter to the Romans: "I am sure that neither death, nor life, nor angels, nor principalities, nor things present, nor things to come, nor powers, nor height, nor depth, nor anything else in all creation, will be able to separate us from the love of God in Christ Jesus our Lord" (Rom 8.38–39).

All of us are fallen human beings, and, as such, we will make mistakes, we will fail. Our stability, coming from this broken, unstable world, may come in admitting our failure in yet another relationship, our inability to persevere in yet another situation and, in that admission, finally turning to ask God to heal and restore what we cannot. Some of us have to face that "here we have no continuing city" in a very real and tangible way. Our way of stability may be to stand before the Lord as literal and spiritual Pilgrims (cf. Mk 6.8–11), preparing ourselves through repentance and prayer for the heavenly Jerusalem that is to come. Nor can those who are given the gift to persevere in family or community assume they are on a higher spiritual plane. If we presume that the gifts and position we are given by grace are ours by right or that we have somehow deserved them, we will find ourselves like the rich man in the Lord's parable who built a barn to horde his wealth only to discover that his life was forfeit (Lk 12.16–21). God's gifts are not given to us so that we may take our ease; they are given so that others may find Him through our lives, deeds and words. Jesus tells us further that "Every one to whom much is given, of him will much be required; and of him to whom men commit much they will demand the more" (Lk 12.48). Even our Orthodox Faith is such a gift (Mt 16.17).

So let us not contemplate our own stability or instability, failures or successes, or those of others. Let us not judge ourselves or one another at all. Rather let us find our strength, our stability and our salvation in God Who alone in infinite love is able to perfect us and those virtues He wills to be ours.

Chapter Ten

PARENTING IN THE CHURCH

*T*HERE IS NO QUESTION that children can survive and grow into wonderful people without proper parenting. There are records of those left to grow up on the street who find the mentoring they need and are able to take their place in "polite society." Such children may even find their way into the Church, although they often have a difficult path, for they have succeeded for the most part by relying on and listening to themselves. The Church is a network of people who rather are obedient: who listen and respond appropriately to one another. Becoming part of such a community where give and take and communication are the norm may be more of a challenge than they want. If they do find the Church, rather than the result of natural growth, it will most probably be a reaction against their situation and the people in their lives.

The kind of parenting, however, that produces children who remain within the Church; who become saints and witnesses to the truth of the Gospel of Christ Jesus, normally begins with parents and grandparents who are themselves men and women of conviction and of prayer. Their obedience, their ability to listen and respond appropriately to Christ and to His Church, is the foundation of their personal lives and of their lives with their spouses. Such obedience is literally response-able when men and women understand the Gospel of Jesus Christ and know it to be a Gospel of love and of freedom. Each person who remains fully in the Church chooses daily to respond in freedom, prayer and action to a God Who loves us so that He gave His only-begotten Son for us. Such Gospel freedom, prayer and action lead us to respond in love to every person and situation God has allowed to be in our presence through the Providence of our daily lives.

Children born within a family with such parents and grandparents will naturally develop a desire for this Gospel life. While they are still very young, their parents and extended family will not need to teach them. Simply their presence will be sufficient, attending to their needs, using words of both loving support and loving correction.

Once children begin speaking and reading, however, another dimension is added to family life. Ours is a literate, sophisticated society where for the most part love is seen either as sex or as smothering, controlling passion. In the Church, however, parents' love for one another and for their children extends beyond this. Rather than controlling each other and their children, they themselves teach or find the necessary teachers so that their children in due time become independent, self-supporting adults, standing solidly on their own feet, equipped to begin their lives apart from their parents.

Such parental teaching within the context of experience is much more than imparting information. It includes helping children, and at times one another, process all that they face as a family and as individuals living in this fallen world. When children are ready, this support and this dialogue over everything from books and teachers to the tragedies they experience themselves or see in the media, is far more important than shielding them from all that is evil and unpleasant. And finally, Christian parents support one another and their children in following God's call, wherever that may take them: training a child at home in the family business; sending him or her off to an apprenticeship, college or university or to the life of a foreign missionary; marriage; seminary or life in a monastery.

Yet the most important part of this parental teaching is living before God. Today we can no longer assume that personal prayer will be absorbed by our children through osmosis. Simply handing our child a prayer book one day will not do the job either. It is a phenomenon of our society even within the Church that parents find it harder to speak with their children about standing before God in prayer than about sex. Both of these are intimate functions of life: the one engenders physical life; the other spiritual life. Each type of life is necessary for the life of the Christian, and the home is normally the place where both kinds of life are to be given.

For Christian parents are adults with a healthy relationship with the Lord. They know that He loves them, and as their Creator, He knows and expects the best of them. They are not afraid to stand before Him and pray in their own words, telling Him of their needs and the needs of their loved ones and thanking Him for their blessings. This is the first and most basic prayer they will teach to their children.

With St. Paul, who tells us to "pray with understanding" (1 Cor 14.15), they read their books of prayer with attention, engaging their heart together with their mind, and bringing themselves before God with their cares. As they pray the Lord's own prayer daily with the phrase "Give us this day our daily bread," they understand that this is more than a prayer for a roof over their heads and three meals a day: The daily bread of the Christian is the life of Jesus Who said: "I am the bread of life; he who comes to me shall not hunger, and he who believes in me shall never thirst" (Jn 6.35).

This prayer is nourished by the life-giving Bread they receive as participants in the Body of Christ in the Mystery of Holy Communion, especially on the Lord's Day each week, and through joining the attendant "Agape," or in modern terms, "Coffee Hour Fellowship" that follows the Eucharist. Secret or personal prayer is the vehicle that carries them through the days and hours spent apart from the physical Body of Christ in the Church. Parents include their children in such liturgical and personal prayer. Children do not usually rebel against such liturgy and prayer unless they see that it does not have results in the daily life of their parents and family, or until they go through the normal individuation process by which they make the faith and life of the Church their own.

Some of us will not be called to be parents of biological children. Nevertheless, as adults, all of us will be called to parenting in one way or another, whether in the "secular" world or within the Church. Indeed, while there are many models for Christian life, that of the family is one of the most basic. St. Paul understands this model when he says, "I became your father in Christ Jesus through the Gospel" (1 Cor 4.13).

As we Christians grow into adulthood, we discover that there are few differences between spiritual and biological parenting. God blesses some families and some parishes with children and adults who have severe physical and mental handicaps so that they need parental supervision throughout their lives; nevertheless, adult children are normally the test of good parenting. St. Paul writes to the Ephesians: "And His gifts were that some should be apostles, some prophets, some evangelists, some pastors and teachers, to equip the saints for the work of ministry, for building up the body of Christ, until *we all* attain to the unity of the faith and of the knowledge of the Son of God, to mature manhood, to the measure of the stature of the fullness of Christ; so that we may no longer be children, tossed to and fro and carried about with every wind of doctrine, by the cunning of men, by their craftiness in deceitful wiles" (Eph 4.11–14, italics added).

While we believe in theory the proverb based on many Gospel texts that as Christians we are to be "in, but not of the world," we need to look at how far removed our actual parenting, both spiritual and biological, may be from that shown to us in the Gospel life of Jesus and the lives of the apostles and saints down the ages. Far too often this parenting in the Church has been lost, swallowed up in a model of hierarchical power, prestige and the service of mammon. I think in such a situation we may safely make our own those words of Jesus, "Call no man 'father' here on earth" (Mt 23.9). This is not just a Protestant proof text; it is the Gospel. However if our fathers and mothers, biological and/or spiritual, are purely earthly, we are called on to look to Jesus; to ask Him in prayer to give us the mentoring we need to fulfill our own adult ministry. If we truly want to follow Him in this way, to grow into ". . . the knowledge of the Son of God, to mature manhood, to the measure of the stature of the fullness of Christ" quoted above, He will give us what we need.

". . . whoever causes one of these little ones who believe in me to sin, it would be better for him to have a great millstone fastened round his neck and to be drowned in the depth of the sea" (Mt 18.6). We would like to believe that although earthly fathers and mothers might lead us into such sin, our official fathers in God would never do so. Writing over a thousand years ago, however, St. John Climacus warns us in his *Ladder of Divine Ascent* to test that one will be under doctors and not sick men; that the ship has a pilot and not just ignorant crew members.[1] Many of us think we can and should bypass this admonition; that it is a sign or test of our piety blindly to submit to the first "spiritual elder" who comes our way. Many times, however, the best mentoring and parenting within the Church comes not from hierarchs, clergy and monastics, but from the men and women in our parishes. These are the faithful who have survived not only natural disasters, economic recessions and family heartache, but also betrayal by bishops, parish priests and monastic elders. Many a family, lacking the ideal Orthodox makeup, has been completed by the parenting of these faithful men and women.

In many parishes today around the world only "Babas" and Yayas" have survived this testing; the men of the parish are conspic-

---

[1]John Climacus, *The Ladder of Divine Ascent*, translated by Colm Luibheid and Norman Russell [Classics of Western Spirituality] (New York: Paulist Press, 1982) p. 92.t

uously absent. Many true spiritual fathers in the priesthood have tales to tell of their own mothers and of the women in their home parishes who taught them, loved them, chastised them and prayed for them. Many of them still look to these mothers in God for their guidance.

Churches and parishes may be simply dysfunctional families, unable to reach out to the equally dysfunctional individuals and families lying, like Lazarus, at their doorsteps, hungry for a crumb of the Gospel they may be hoarding for themselves in one way or another (cf. Lk 16). As the rich man ignored Lazarus, many parishes ignore those in need. We may keep our Gospel wealth, for example, hidden under a language we ourselves do not understand. If we are a bishop or a priest, rather than having the confidence to reach out to and parent those clergy and faithful given to our charge, we may instead hide behind our own inadequacies and rather demand from them respect and support, financial and otherwise. "I will not be a burden, for I seek not what is yours but you; for children ought not to lay up for their parents, but parents for their children," says St. Paul to the Corinthians (2 Cor 12.14). This is the voice of an adult parent.

Rather than becoming disciples, many parishioners believe their role in church is to be seen as children, kept at a distance and properly disciplined. This model of parish life is like the worst of Victorian nurseries. Instead of getting to know his parishioners on more than a social level, nurturing and educating at least some of them to mature adulthood in Christ, to a share in the ministry and outreach of the parish so that every soul within the parish and every possible convert is touched and brought the healing Word of Christ, a priest may hold the riches of his seminary education to himself, in effect emasculating himself rather than becoming a parent. St Peter tells all of us, not just the hierarchs, clergy and monastics, that we are like living stones, to be built ourselves into a spiritual house, to be a holy priesthood, to offer spiritual sacrifices acceptable to God through Jesus Christ (cf. 1 Pet 2.5).

We may point to our own allegedly pious obedience to "holy tradition" and "spiritual fathers" for these deformed views of discipleship and ministry. Where the Orthodox Church, her hierarchs, clergy and faithful have developed traditions that are in direct conflict to the Gospel commands of Jesus and his apostles, however, such obedience is rather the blind obedience of the Pharisee to the traditions that are of man and not of God.

There may be many true models for Church life. Let us reject any that undermine or supplant the model of the family and the role of parents, both spiritual and biological. As in the monastic life, all life-professed monks and nuns are called "Mother" and "Father," let each one of us, no matter what our calling, no matter how badly our own parents, spiritual or biological, may seem to have failed us, be willing to grow into his or her own responsibility as an adult parent, knowing that God gives us the love, wisdom, strength and courage we need.

Chapter Eleven

THE SOUL AND HEALTH

*W*E HUMANS HAVE a soul that is expressed here and now in our physical body. While the fate of the souls of other created beings may be a matter of conjecture, as Christians, we believe that after death has separated our soul from our body, they will be reunited at the Resurrection and thus united, we will live eternally before God.

However, we do not believe that the body as we have it now in time and space will inherit eternal life: St. Paul tells us that our resurrectional body will be as different from our physical body as an oak tree is from an acorn (1 Cor 15.36–44). And we know that when we speak of eternity we are speaking of a reality that is beyond time and space and thus totally beyond the powers of our wildest imaginations. Any concept of God and the Kingdom of Heaven that we can come up with is simply a human construct and the terms of apophatic theology: "inconceivable, indescribable, incomprehensible . . ." are far more accurate.

Nevertheless, for us the body is inextricably linked with the soul and any attempts to separate them, even in thought and word, are artificial. Death is terrible for us because it is the sundering of two things that are meant to be united. A bodiless soul is the ghost of a human being, the antithesis of saints who even after death have been seen here on earth in their resurrection bodies, more alive and radiant than any of us can be now, although some saints, such as St. Seraphim of Sarov, have been seen to shine with the uncreated light of God's energies even during their earthly lives.

While both religion and science tell us that our body and our soul are inextricably linked, in our belief that the soul is also attuned to the spirit, we part company with science. No matter how badly damaged our bodies may be physically, as long as our souls are not parted from them by death there is still room for the spirit to act.

So the spirit is where we enter the realm of warfare between good and evil. Just as surely as our souls and bodies are created and sustained by God's Holy Spirit, so also on this earth are they subject to fallen spirits. None of creation can exist apart from God, even though within the limits of created time and space, as our loving Parent, when we so choose, He lets us go off on our own to learn our own lessons. The snake that slithered into Paradise portrays the biblical intuition that mankind is neither alone nor first in such a choice: existing evil invited Adam and Eve to choose an alternative to God's reality. God does not force His presence where it is not desired, then or now.

So for us, sickness and health are not simply a matter of catching germs that make us ill and taking pills to make us get well. While I do not deny the reality of germs and the efficacy of medicines, I see them as parts of God's creation, good in so far as they participate in the life of God and are not set up by us humans as idols apart from God, taking on a life of their own, becoming demonic and destructive.

What is the basis of health? What are we to do when it leaves us and we find ourselves in a state of dis-ease? How then do we find healing? These are questions that all of us will have to face at one time or another, and some more than others in this life.

For us as Christians, health is much more than the simple absence of physical disease. We believe that a person's immortal soul may be very healthy even though their physical body is being destroyed by disease or some other malady. We would say further that a person can be very well adjusted emotionally to their circumstances, have robust physical health and still be sick in soul.

It is interesting to note that today many people equate "getting sick" or having an infirmity of one kind or another with sin. No matter how often we have heard the Lord's answer to those who questioned Him: "Who sinned: This man or his parents that he was born blind?" (Jn 9.22). We just know that if that person were in harmony with himself, or took care of himself properly, he would not get sick nor would he produce a defective offspring. This is taken to its logical conclusion by parents who will abort children they know are less than perfect. Bringing a handicapped or "special" child to birth is now added to the contemporary list of unforgivable sins. Only beautiful people need apply to be born today.

All the elements of creation can choose to take things into their own hands and survive seemingly on their own without reference to God, but when such a mode of existence is chosen, divine love and freedom are increasingly missing. We cannot exist without community, which must include communion with God as well as with our fellow humans and the rest of creation. We must nurture a small child in spirit as well as in body for it to flourish. It will die if either one is completely neglected. An adult may be able to live cut off completely from community, but its soul will be shriveled, and common wisdom tells us that it will become a strange being.

Real discernment may be needed to see this pattern in our lives. If we neglect the spiritual aspect of our souls, seeking to feed only on physically healthy food and drink while cutting ourselves off from the Food and Drink of Eternal Life in communion with the Body and Blood of Christ in the Eucharist as well as with His Body that is the Church, we will not have the eyes to see, the ears to hear, or the heart to understand the true realities of our life. Where sickness of soul leads us to sickness of body, we may prefer to take a pill rather than to forgive others and receive healing forgiveness ourselves. Where physical health could lead us to the service of others and the glory of God, it may instead lead us to acquire and save up material possessions and wealth that corrupt us and lead us to sickness of soul, keeping us from spending all that we are and all that we have to purchase the eternal pearl of great price.

We have this understanding if the eyes of our heart are set on God, eternity and the Kingdom of Heaven. A soul that is preparing to enter into these realities will not be entirely wedded to this earth. On the contrary, it will be looking towards death as the necessary gate to life and will choose to see the present in the light of God's eternity. This vision will not be morbid and sick: God's love calls all into eternal being, and the call to eternal life is not less than our initial birth into the life of this earth. Following Christ, we are to live fully here on earth, not seeking death before our time. Yet when our time comes, as it came for Him, we should pray for the grace to lay down our lives, accepting whatever suffering and death God sets out as our personal path to the Resurrection.

Chapter Twelve
MARY AND MARTHA

*T*HE ORTHODOX CHURCH will always provide difficulties for fundamentalists. We have far too much poetry, far too many "good stories," including those told by the Lord Himself, far too many loose associations in the writings of our people over the last two thousand years or so to satisfy those who would prefer religion to be proclaimed by a precise and complete video camera documentary of all that has happened from the first moment of Creation.

Our Orthodox approach to Mary, the Theotokos, and Mary and Martha, the Myrrhbearers and sisters of Lazarus, is no exception. The "common" Gospel reading for feasts of the Theotokos blatantly conflates Mary, the Mother of Jesus with Mary, the sister of Lazarus: "Jesus entered a village; and a woman named Martha received him into her house. And she had a sister called Mary, who sat at the Lord's feet and listened to his teaching. But Martha was distracted with much serving; and she went to him and said, 'Lord, do you not care that my sister has left me to serve alone? Tell her then to help me.' But the Lord answered her, 'Martha, Martha, you are anxious and troubled about many things; one thing is needful. Mary has chosen the good portion, which shall not be taken away from her.' As he said this, a woman in the crowd raised her voice and said to him, 'Blessed is the womb that bore you, and the breasts that you sucked!' But he said, 'Blessed rather are those who hear the word of God and keep it!'" (Lk 10.38–42, 11.27–28).

I want to begin by looking at Mary and Martha of Bethany. I've always had a hunch that in this story, before the Lord arrived, Mary was right there with Martha getting all the food ready and cleaning the house. Martha's problem was that she didn't know how to enjoy her parties. I'm going to guess that Mary was a good hostess, the kind who prepares everything ahead so that when the guests arrive she can sit down and enjoy them. Martha was sure her guests needed to be waited on hand and foot. The Lord rightly reprimanded her for that. Martha's error is one many of us fall into, especially if, like me, we tend to be task-oriented. We want everyone to think that we are perfect and so we go out of our way doing things that don't need to be done. While we may gain the satisfaction of seeing tasks or projects completed, we can sometimes lose companionship and love along the way.

Because of this story, Mary has come to stand for the contemplative life, the main reason why she and Mary the Mother of God are often conflated; Martha stands for the active life. However, when we talk this way, we are taking one small episode in the lives of these sisters out of context. We are assuming that Martha spent her entire life fussing over serving and Mary was always sitting down listening. Tradition, however, tells us that both women went on to be Myrrhbearers; very old local traditions in both Southern France and England hold that both came with their brother Lazarus as apostles and evangelists. In St. John's Gospel, Martha is the one who makes the same confession of faith as Peter: "You are the Christ, the Son of the Living God." The Lord taught her a lesson and she learned it. Right there we have a very good reason to emulate her.

I believe we should emulate both women, whether we want to or not. The most austere, contemplative, "angelic" monastery is made up of men or women who are definitely human beings. We find stories in the very early Desert Fathers and Mothers of people coming to the monastery and being scandalized when they are asked to help with work. They would inform the abbot or abbess that they had come to be holy and to pray. So the story goes that they are shown to a room and allowed to pray. But also not called when it is time for meals or brought even bread and water. In the desert heat, it takes less than a day before humans feel that they are not quite up to this aspect of angelic life. Saint Paul tells us that those who choose not to work should not eat. On an empty stomach, work begins to look good.

So really, for humans in general and Christians in particular, there is no such thing as strict contemplation versus complete activity. There are people who cannot work—infants, or invalids through sickness or old age—and for them, growing or healing or preparing for death are indeed full-time occupations. For the rest of us, balance is the key to life.

I have often heard a complaint, especially from young priests' wives who volunteered for that job not only because they loved the man they married but also because they love God and the Church and wanted to have a life closer to them, that instead of living this wonderful life of constant Church services and prayer and perhaps even serving the poor and otherwise rescuing mankind, they are home changing diapers, wiping dripping noses, listening to complaints from parishioners that they and their husband are not holy (or neat, or stylish) enough (or too holy, too neat, too stylish . . .). I am used to novices in the monastery with similar complaints. We have a farm at our monastery. But even if we didn't, we have the monastery and guest house to clean, meals to prepare, lawns to mow in the summer and snow to plow in the winter, bills to pay and finances to track without a regular income (heaven help us these days if our bookkeeping is not "transparent"), furnaces, plumbing and roofs that need maintenance . . . and no husbands or teenage sons handy to help with these things. In addition, we are the ones solely responsible for making sure that services are sung in our chapel on a regular, daily basis, usually without benefit of a priest.

So how do we manage still to be nuns? How do some presvyteras, panis and matushki arrive at a ripe old age as loving, shining Christians? How can we be both Marys and converted Marthas, able to make the confession that Jesus is the Lord in our lives as well?

We need to be fed with the Word of God in both Scripture and Sacraments, but if that food does not give us the eyes to see and the hands to work and the hearts to love whomever and whatever God wills to send us each day in His providence, then something is missing. Because truly, the Christian life and therefore the monastic life and the life of a presvytera or matushka or pani and her family is nothing other than learning to live one day at a time before God, accepting that He allows whatever happens to be for our salvation. This can seem hard. Yet how little we have been tested! How would it have been—or how will it be if some terrorists manage to succeed in some of their plans—if we were to be faced with the choice of giving up everyone and everything we love or denying Christ? Literally thousands of nuns in the twentieth century were martyred and thousands more matushki watched their parish churches being vandalized and burned and their husbands being beaten, tortured, shot or led away to certain death in Russia. Presvyteras went through the same thing for centuries in what is now modern Turkey and in Greece down to the time of their war for independence and then again under the Nazi occupation. Those living in parts of Eastern Europe, the Middle East, Asia and Africa face such testing to this very day.

We do not have the choice to spend 24 hours in Church. We do have to choose to take the spiritual, mental and physical nourishment we need in God's providence to live the lives we have chosen. And indeed it is true that "not to decide is to decide." This means learning that we have choices about saying "No" to certain things around us. Far too many people today seem to feel they have no choice—they "must" watch television, play computer games, make sure their children get to every sports or school event, you name it—

forced more surely to this sort of a culture than if someone were holding a gun to their head. And of course, if one feels that way, there will be no room for prayer, for time spent together as a family at home or in Church, for learning about the faith and the men and women who have gone before us and become saints, born into this world as surely as we are.

Here is where I think it is helpful to follow tradition and add Mary, the Mother of God to these thoughts. When I was young I was a bit uncomfortable with some of the language about Mary that I encountered in what I could see of the Roman Catholic Church and later the Orthodox churches. This does not mean that I did not have veneration for her. A surprising number of Protestants—especially those who pray and have read their Bibles—have a very real love and veneration for her. My grandmother, who was raised a good Lutheran, loved to recite the *Magnificat* and believed it was fitting that "all generations" should "call her blessed." I was raised an Episcopalian and when I "got religion" as a teenager and entered the convent, I had my initial monastic training in the Episcopal Community of St. Mary whose patron is the Mother of God.

The veneration for St. Mary that I was taught then was what I would call sober and practical. In one of the first conversations I remember having with my novice mistress, she said that we would find in her our best example of becoming a Christian and therefore a nun and a handmaid of the Lord. In commenting on St. Luke's story of the Annunciation, she pointed out that immediately after hearing the news from the Archangel Gabriel that she would be the Mother of God, her response was to go to stay with her cousin Elizabeth who was then in her sixth month of pregnancy. Luke tells us that she stayed there for three months – in other words, it seems she went to be with her and probably help out until the baby was born.

Underneath all the flowery poetry the Orthodox Church has heaped upon Mary, I believe that same sober and practical veneration for her remains. After all, she is so important in the Church—and in the whole of creation—precisely because her very real created humanity received the fullness of God. St. Cyril of Alexandria at the Council of Ephesus fought for her title "Theotokos" in order to make sure that the Church can never forget that our Lord God and Savior Jesus Christ was born as a human infant to a real human mother. That may not seem so important to our rationalistic, scientific world view, but earlier generations had no trouble believing in divinities and spirits. They had more of a problem accepting that God could walk this earth as a human person. I think, on the practical level, we still do have a touch of this. Most of us are pretty schizophrenic when we look at it—we have one way of relating to our "real world" and another way of thinking and feeling when we move into our religious mode. Being able to get it all together, to see Mary as both a wife and mother whose feet were planted as firmly on the ground as we might like to think ours are, and at the same time realizing that she was and is indeed "more honorable than the cherubim and beyond compare more glorious than the seraphim" and that as she brought God into the world, her "womb became more spacious than the heavens" is really a bit of a stretch for us.

I think it is important to work on stretching like this, though. I think Mary is the way to God for us, as she always has been since that memorable day when she met the Archangel Gabriel. And I believe that in her own person, she combined very well the two "Mary and Martha" vocations of contemplation and activity. I believe it is very important to have a healthy relationship with her as our spiritual mother. With Mary, we realize that in a very real sense, God needs women. He set up His creation in such a way that He could not enter it as a man without a woman. When one tries to throw Mary out, one is left, as many Protestants are, with the impression of a God who can do just fine without women, thank you. There are some within the Orthodox Church as well who have this attitude, and it can lead, for example, to those who believe the Church needs only spiritual fathers; that everything is about power. If they are the ones with that power, they should rule the Church, and if they do not have that power, they should challenge those who do. It may never even occur to such people that women (and in many cases, laymen as well) can or should be taken into account and given more to do than show up for services, bake pieroghis or baklava, clean the church and sew buttons on cassocks.

Provided women continue to be mothers, spiritual motherhood is a reality that is very much needed in the Church. Women can also be excellent administrators and task completers, for example, and hopefully we can avoid classic male roles such as taking sides and rooting for parties. We need to become saints: While monks in this country are frequently named after American saints, we can't do the same with our nuns; as yet there are no recognized female American saints.

Many of the so-called (and sometimes rightly so-called) oppressive patriarchal attitudes in the Church are relatively late developments in the Orthodox world. Historically, we know widows and deaconesses had official ministries in the Church for hundreds of years. We nuns who serve at the altar in our own chapels and do some teaching are the remnants of part of that practice. St. Elizabeth, the Grand Duchess and New Martyr of Russia, very consciously revived the aspect of the serving diaconate when she founded her order of deaconesses in the early 20th century. A deaconess is different from a deacon, and I am not advocating that we be ordained as clergy—that is a whole other issue. I will say, though, that I think the desire to have women priests that we find even among some Orthodox comes in large part from the vacuum that has been created by the exclusion of women (and laymen) from legitimate ministries.

In the United States I believe there is an added element: The rush to become "American" by many Orthodox has translated into accepting the Protestant world view, including that approach to the Mother of God and the other saints. I have heard Orthodox priests leave out "Most Holy Theotokos, save us" during services. Yet they are not troubled by hearing of a fireman or a doctor who saves people. The saints are the first to remind us that they can do nothing by themselves; that any gifts they have and can share come from God and are given to lead us back to salvation in God.

Mary stands as a strong corrective to all of our wrong impressions. We should remember that while, like Martha, she was not averse to serving as a handmaid, she also stands in prayer with "the other Mary" and has the glory and honor of Queen of all creation. We too are called to serve, as St. Paul puts it in his letter to the Ephesians: "He who descended is He Who also ascended far above all the heavens, that He might fill all things. And His gifts were that some should be apostles, some prophets, some evangelists, some pastors and teachers, to equip the saints for the work of ministry, for building up the body of Christ, until we all attain to the unity of the faith and of the knowledge of the Son of God, to mature manhood, to the measure of the stature of the fullness of Christ . . . " (4.10–13).

In the light of our many and varied callings to prayer and service in the Church and in the world, let us be inspired to seek Mary, the Mother of Jesus, together with Mary and Martha of Bethany, whom she undoubtedly knew. These three women continue to be here with us as strong, active and praying presences, challenging our view of ourselves as well as our view of them and of our God.

Chapter Thirteen

DOUBT AND PRAYER

An interview with Carla Zell of Conciliar Press for
The Handmaiden *magazine, Vol. 12, No. 1, Winter 2008.*
Used with permission.

Carla: I have a list of questions women have asked me over the years. My guess is that many women are hesitant to verbalize their doubts (wanting to appear "spiritual," even when they don't feel they really are), and would be comforted to realize that they are not alone in experiencing such doubts and tests of their faith. My guess is also that many of our women readers would appreciate the advice of an abbess in such matters, and would likely trust the answers more than if such an article was written by a wife or mother living in the world. Here are some of the questions:

How to deal with little doubts that flit through our minds "from out of the blue," like little darts, questioning whether what we believe is true;

How to deal with doubts that nag at us when our prayers are seemingly not answered, that make us wonder whether we trust and believe in God and the power of prayer as much as we should;

How to deal with doubts that afflict us when we are faced with adversity in our lives, that cause us to question why God would allow such things in our lives, or how a good God could allow bad things to happen in the world;

How to deal with doubts that trouble our faith intellectually, arising from conversations with non-believers or other Christians who question our beliefs system?

MR: In my mind, these four questions about thoughts can be lumped together under one category. If as Christians we don't have these particular questions, we will have others that challenge our faith and, if we are left to our own devices, they will cause us to blaspheme God, leave the Church and/or the faith (we can stay in the Church and pretend, or we can leave the Church and have our own private religion). Further, sometimes they can also lead us to justify leaving our spouses if they continue to believe. These thoughts tend to come especially at times when we are vulnerable from stress or illness, for example, but they can also assault us in broad daylight when "everything's going my way."

I believe there is only one remedy for them. Such thoughts and questions come from delusion, so while it's a good idea to keep reading the Scriptures and sound books on the faith, prayer is absolutely essential and is the key to coming out on the other side with one's life, faith and membership in the Body of Christ intact. Without a living relationship with God and His saints, all the right ideas in the world won't make a difference.

This means much more than just "saying prayers," although that is a start. I know there are spiritual teachers who will claim that one should pray only by reading the prayers in prayer books. I disagree with that. If the saints had done that, there would be no prayers in our prayer books! And we need to remember that Orthodox Christians have been praying much longer than mass-produced prayer books have been available. We have to find our heart, however we may do that—and many times we have to begin such prayer simply by asking God and the saints for help in finding our heart and learning to pray. The prayers in prayer books can indeed help us to keep our heads screwed on straight and we should use them—I must confess that one time when I was struggling myself with some theological issues, a phrase in one of St. Basil's prayers that I regularly read as part of my preparation for communion suddenly jumped out of the page and was the answer for me. The bothersome thoughts didn't go away instantly, but I found that with time, as I repeated St. Basil's phrase each time the thoughts came, they finally gave up. I felt this was a real way in which St. Basil was present with me and I have found myself turning to him ever since whenever theological doubts have surfaced in my mind.

I think this discovery that the saints are alive, well, and present with us has been one of the most powerful factors in my own life in the Church. We cannot make it into heaven on our own. If we aren't members of the Body of Christ, alive to all the other members, including especially those who have gone before us, who have "fought the good fight and received their crowns," then we are like branches cut off a tree and left lying on the ground to wither and die. Many of us are converts who were raised with the idea that there is something wrong with praying to the saints—we should just go to the head, not bother with the underlings in the organization. Well, even in real life that doesn't work. When we speak with others (including the saints who are not present physically to us) we do so knowing that we speak in the presence of God. If we never speak to His saints, He may not recognize us as part of His organization.

So when doubts and troubling thoughts of whatever kind come, we should become a bit child-like, as we must anyway, to enter the Kingdom of Heaven. We can begin with our guardian angel and our patron saint and if they aren't the ones who can lead us to the answer, we ask them to send us the saint(s) who will. This may sound silly and it may feel silly and artificial at first. But things begin to happen when we really turn to the saints and ask their help. God Himself acts powerfully through them and we can then turn to Him in gratitude for His help.

I've written about this before, and while it feels a little strange to quote myself, when I don't have anything new to say, I'd best admit the fact : "We also need help with the thoughts and feelings that bombard us both from outside and within our own heads and hearts. The fathers and mothers of the Church tell us that we will never get away from such thoughts and feelings; they always will be there. This is again where simple prayer—a verse from the Psalms, "Lord, have mercy," the Lord's name—whatever seems right for us—can be used, almost like a tennis racket to hit the distracting feelings and thoughts away. As long as we can do this—as long as we can separate ourselves from them for even a brief moment—we are not held captive by them. And that little space we create each time we "hit" such a thought or feeling with the name of the Lord or some other brief prayer, gives God all the room He needs to act in our lives. We simply learn not to be bothered by the fact that thoughts and feelings are there (p. 85 "Climbing the Spiritual Ladder" in *Growing in Christ, Shaped in His Image,* published by St. Vladimir's Seminary Press. 2003

C: Here is another—how to deal with growing apathy in our lives, when we start to ask ourselves "are our attempts to live a Christian life, go to church, and pray worth the struggle?"

MR: This is a different type of question. Here we have to look at our lives as a whole and ask ourselves some serious questions in turn. Am I apathetic about life as a whole? Or is it just my life in Christ? If I'm feeling really energetic and raring to go in every other aspect of my life, then I should shake myself well and force myself to get back into harness and start pulling my load again, even if I think my own particular share of Christ's sufferings is more than I can carry. And the advice given above then applies to this situation as well.

However if we're apathetic about everything, then we may have a physical, mental or emotional, rather than a spiritual problem. We may need to talk with a doctor about our health. Or we may just need to start eating well, getting enough sleep at night, and making sure we get some good exercise several times a week. But when one is very sick, there is a type of praying one cannot do. And God does not ask it from us. We just have to let go and as best we can, when we can, ask Him and His saints for healing, and let them do the praying for us. There are people with physical, mental, and emotional weaknesses and/or illnesses who are never going to be giants in some kinds of prayer, and may never even be well enough to get to church. Yet if they can learn humility through their suffering and not lose the sense that even at their worst, even when God feels a million miles away, He is still there, God accepts this. He has allowed this suffering for their salvation and will not abandon them.

C: A final one—how can we help our children regain their faith if they stray away from church in high school or when they go to college?

MR: We cannot do anything to help our children regain their faith if they stray away from Church as they grow up. Once our children have grown, we have to let go of them and let them lead their own lives and make their own choices and decisions. Whether we have raised them well (and the biggest part of that is giving them an example by the way we have lived our lives and spoken our words), whether we have made huge mistakes that we must learn to repent of before God and His people, or whether we have raised them well along with some mistakes, what is left to us is prayer. Prayer is not trying to manipulate our children from a distance—perhaps even thinking that God and His saints are more powerful manipulators than we are if we can get them on our side. Prayer is taking the time and making the space regularly in our lives to put our children (and all of our loved ones) in God's hands; asking the saints for their help in doing this; asking their guardian angels and their saints to be there with them. Prayer is letting go and trusting God. Such prayer is also a powerful statement to our children that we trust them. As long as we are taking the time and making the space to rescue them, we are giving them an equally powerful message that we think they are still children, incapable of handling whatever it may be.

Will our children always "turn out right?" No. Especially not on our schedule. But if we truly pray, if we truly love God, then we give them the best possible atmosphere to choose what is good and true, even when it does not seem right to us. And they will know that we love them, no matter what. This is the way God loves. For some of us, part of the Cross we may be asked to carry is to share in the suffering He endures each time one of us turns away from Him in order to pursue our own self-willed agenda.

Overall, the best thing we can do for ourselves and our children (and for all of our loved ones) is really to learn and understand that we are always, wholly, totally in the presence of God no matter what we do or say, no matter what we endure or perpetrate. Whether or not we recognize His presence, we cannot get away from Him. If we accept this presence and the great love that He has offered us and will always offer us, even now we have a foretaste of heaven. This is a simple understanding, but it is the basis on which all theology and prayer rests. Any words of theology and prayer apart from this realization are simply "noisy gongs and clanging cymbals" (1 Cor 13.1). When we make the time and the space, with God we acquire the love of the Holy Spirit, and as St. Seraphim teaches us, then God can save thousands around us.

Chapter Fourteen

AS GOD WILLS

Commencement Address at St Vladimir's Seminary, May 2009

IT IS POSSIBLE TO BE a member of the Orthodox Church, graduate from a seminary, perhaps even be a member of the clergy or other full-time Church professional, and not believe in God or in His providence. I would like to tackle this reality.

I suggest that there is a God; that He is everything He is cracked up to be by all the theology that is taught in our seminaries and preached in our churches; that whether or not we see Him working in history in the same way that the Biblical writers have seen Him work, He is the living, active and personal Source of all that has being.

And that being includes us at this very moment as we sit and read, listen or dream, or tune out our surroundings by calling someone on a cell phone.

If this is true—and I challenge all of you to put Him to that test—then it follows that a relationship with Him is probably a good idea and something we ought not to leave to our Baptist brethren.

I know that there are all sorts of approaches to liturgy, worship and prayer. What I have learned, sadly, over the years, however, is that many people use liturgy, prayers, prayer books, prayer ropes—all sorts of paraphernalia that have come to be associated with various forms of religious expression—for many reasons other than forming a relationship with the God and Father of our Lord Jesus Christ. I have learned that when I am asked to speak with people—any people—I can take nothing for granted in this department.

Now I add a side note that I want to weave into this discussion. I simply quote a conversation that I have had, word for word, mul-

tiple times over during the thirty plus years I have been an Orthodox nun.

"Mother, why are the American monasteries, or why is your own
monastery so small."

"Father, who in your parish is being prepared for this life."

I seriously do not want the Church to hire someone to design
posters advertising monastic vocations to place on parish bulletin
boards, although I wouldn't object to a line or two added to one or
another litanies praying not only for our "brotherhood in Christ" but
for male and female monastics around the world.

But I suggest rather that, as is taught, the monastic life is a result
of the "*bene esse*," the well-being of the Church. When monastic life
is flourishing, it is because the Church is healthy. Small and belea-
guered monasteries, monastics struggling with the wrong things, are
a sign that something is wrong with our Church environment as
surely as frogs showing bizarre mutations, strange diseases and simple disappearance from our landscape show that the world's environment is poisoned.

There have been and are cultures where as young people seek to
discern God's will for their lives, monasticism is considered one
healthy choice among others. But we have a culture, even a "church"
culture, where the phrase "As God Wills," signifies a negative, fatal-
istic approach to life, and who in their right mind would try to find
that for any future?

I have learned to use this phrase from my Arab Palestinian
friends, most of whom are Christian. Nevertheless, influenced by the
Moslem culture around them, some seem unaware of St. Paul's
words: "Work out your own salvation, knowing that God is working
within you" (Phil 2.12–13).

Two things are operative here—two persons working out salvation. There is God Who is creating reality, allowing universes, galax-

ies, black holes, solar systems and our tiny planet earth to exist, allowing us our brief time on this strange planet earth, allowing me to be writing these words, allowing you to read them in this present moment— in other words, allowing us simply to be. In the place beyond space and the time beyond time where God exists, you and I each have an eternity to stand face to face with Him and in a personal relationship, grow eternally with Him into our personal reality.

It has been the teaching of our Church down the millennia that how we use this small portion of created time and space we call our life matters incredibly. Perhaps if we are angels, principalities, or powers, it is different, for they already traverse the created universe in ways that we cannot imagine. We are human beings, and precisely because we are human beings, we are made in the image and likeness of God in a way no other creatures have been.

For this reason—that you and I have been created as human beings—we are persons. And if in some way each of us identifies with the definition of an Orthodox Christian person, we cannot see our God simply as the New Age "Force" behind creation, but as the three Persons in Whose Image we are formed. Moreover, since Jesus walked this earth, we see the second Person of the Trinity as a very human Person, both God and Man.

One of St. John's Epistles tells us that if we are Christians, we will walk as He walked. Many of us Orthodox Christians cringe at the idea of wearing bracelets or whatever with the letters: WWJD, "What Would Jesus Do," now being worn by many Protestants. Yet we need to ask ourselves why we cringe at this. A very Orthodox writer of Scripture said, "Walk as He walked" (1 Jn 2.6). Yet perhaps there is something to cringe at: Whether we like it or not, we are in the hands of the Living God and that is a fearful thing. However much we need to get to know God through the Man Jesus Christ,

He is not our buddy. He is our Friend, and that is a very different matter.

As Orthodox Christians, we are to learn to find our heart, the center of our being, if you will, our *nous*. We are to explore our relationship with our God more seriously than we could or might explore any other relationship in our lives, whether that be as lover, friend, or co-worker. We do not dismiss the inclusion by the old Rabbis of *The Song of Songs* in the Bible. Each of us sees God as our Lover or Spouse, or our relationships with any other lover or spouse will be idolatry.

What does this mean? It does not mean neglecting our spouse, our sisters and brothers, our children, our friends and co-workers, or the rest of our lives so that we may think about God or say prayers all the time. It certainly does not mean having a warm fuzzy feeling or even theological understanding that God is here, all the time. None of these is at the basis of prayer without ceasing, a healthy monastic vocation, or the vocation of any Christian, either lay or clergy, all called to be the holy priesthood of our God in this world.

We all know that lovers usually begin with physical closeness and awareness, quality time in appropriate places, private exploration and discovery. We also know that something is wrong with a relationship if one cannot eventually let one's lover out of one's sight. I am rather to allow those times and places of physical closeness and awareness to change me.

Those of you who are happily married know that your relationship gives you the support you need to go out into the world each day and do your very best at whatever it is you are doing. You cannot be thinking about your spouse every moment: you must be putting your thoughts and efforts into your studies, your job, your children, your clients, whatever else you do. Your relationship stabilizes you. It does not define you, rather you and your spouse support one another in growing into whomever and whatever God in His infinite wisdom allows, calls you to be.

Our relationship with God alone defines us. If we are Orthodox Christians, we acknowledge our God as the most important Person in our lives.

This is where I think many, many Orthodox Christians are functionally atheists or at best new-agers. Do we treat God with a rudeness that allows us to wake up, hear the radio music, smell the coffee and check our e-mails before, if we are in a pious mood, we nod in His direction? Far too often we act as if God is not there, or is not there as a Person, the One Who is everywhere and fills all things. When we can go whole days not speaking to Him, to someone we know is in the same house with us, we should know that our relationship is in trouble.

We are called to be changed by God's reality. We are called to use liturgy and personal prayer in all their forms as lovers use quality time with their beloved, to deepen and form a relationship that allows us to be our true selves—especially, when we are not in the felt, physical presence of the beloved.

This is as God wills. This is who we are when we face the terrifying reality of God who says to us: "I have called you friends" (Jn 15.15). To be a friend is to have infinite responsibility placed on one's shoulders. To be a friend is to become a co-worker. To be a friend means treating every person—including oneself—with the infinite respect one gives the children of valued friends and co-workers.

To be a friend is to acknowledge our Friend, our co-worker, even when we may feel He has abandoned us, as Jesus was abandoned on the Cross. This should not surprise us. "If anyone would be My disciple, let him take up his cross and follow Me" (Mt 16.24). Mother Teresa of Calcutta walked where many, many of the friends of Christ have walked, allowing her life to be formed by the reality she had experienced as a young lover of God, even when it seemed He had abandoned her.

We are made in the image and likeness of a God Who is the great storyteller. How we each will live out our lives, our existence as created beings, will depend upon the stories we tell ourselves and others. If we think we are not telling stories, we tell a story about ourselves.

For instance, there are the basic, negative stories we tell ourselves: "I can't do it." "I don't feel well." "I'm sick." "It's too hard for me." "It's their fault." "I can't help it." If we tell ourselves these little stories over and over, day after day, they will indeed become our story.

There are other stories: "I can do anything I want to do." "I can have anything I want." "I can use anyone I want to use."

All of these stories have one thing in common: they are based in our human reality apart from God. To begin to live as God wills, we must place ourselves within God's reality. We must repeat to ourselves until we literally get by heart the Gospel story, the story of good news for the poor, healing for the sick, eyes for the blind, life for the lifeless, hope for the hopeless; and we must place ourselves within that story. We must play out daily the actions and words before us as surely as any novelist or screenwriter, again and again bringing ourselves and those around us back before the possibility of God whose will is true, alive, and active. Placing ourselves within His will does not artificially limit us; rather by opening the door to humility, it allows us to accept our true God-given limitations and thus to grow into our honest God-given potential.

Much of our responsibility as adults, as parents or teachers, parish priests, healers and care-givers, office workers and professionals, builders or artists, lies in our God-given ability to tell and interpret the story of those around us.

If one day follows another with boring regularity and increasing vulnerability to economic downturns, do we understand how each day He sustains us, gives us our daily bread? Do we accept His blessing for the poor in spirit and, with St. Paul, learn to rejoice in the story of our poverty as well as we did in our wealth?

Has our parish church burned down? How we interpret that disaster to our people, to our bishop, will create the future, or the demise, of our congregation.

Has a friend won the lottery? Can we help him or her stay grounded with a story that has a future with family and friends?

Has a family been visited with disastrous death or long-term illness? How do we help that family with their story? Will we feed them platitudes, or the darkness of our own need and despair? Will we know rather when to stand back and support them as they live their own story through such times?

I share here what I find personally useful so that I can live in the present moment, remembering the past and looking towards the future.

I have learned that when I find myself looking at people and situations, whether remembering the past or looking at this present moment which soon will be past, seeing everyone and everything in a very clear light, my voice laying bare the evil, the limitations, the sin, the ugliness, the falsity, the wrongness around me with mocking accuracy, then I am seeing with demonic eyes and telling the story that the devil has told since before the beginning of the world. There are variations on this theme: I see the past, everyone I knew in the past, and myself in the midst with a rosy glow softening the edges and soft music playing in the background. The demonic clarity with which I see the present and those in it becomes an even more devastating vision of condemnation. Then of course another variation: I see myself and my present friends with great love and deep understanding. We are the wave of the present and the future and I see that all the past individuals and institutions who created the mess we are in were poor helpless idiots whose ideas and designs must be overturned and thwarted if I am to get God's will done on earth.

The Book of Job is our guide here. It is the devil's role to be the accuser of our brethren. Every one of us, whatever our position in or relationship to the Church, needs to be very careful not to be the ones who do his work for him. We are called to see Christ within one another; we are called to create Paradise for ourselves and others even when we find ourselves in the midst of the worst hell of a concentration camp, a gulag, a parish, a family, work, school, any situation. When we demonize—or idolize—any individual or situation, and here I would say especially our own personal past and those who people it, we are creating a false story.

As our stories are true, we will begin to see that they come together as His story. May we want, may we love both the story of our own lives and of His reality. May we find ourselves and one another, every one of us, rejoicing as it is written, seated together in eternity as the spouse, the Bride of Christ, at the Marriage Supper of the Lamb.

This is indeed As God Wills.